GENESIS

THE CLASSIC BIBLE BOOKS SERIES

GENESIS
The Book of Beginnings

Abridged from the text of the Revised English Bible

INTRODUCED AND EDITED BY LAWRENCE BOADT
FOREWORD BY SARA MAITLAND

St. Martin's Griffin
New York

ISBN 0-312-22104-5 paperback

Library of Congress Cataloging-in-Publication Data

Genesis : the book of beginnings / abridged from the text of the
    Revised English Bible / foreword by Sara Maitland ; introduction by
    Lawrence Boadt.
        p.   cm. -- (The Classic Bible Series)
    Includes bibliographical references and index.
    ISBN 0-312-22104-5
    1. Bible. O.T. Genesis--Criticism, interpretation, etc.
I. Boadt, Lawrence. II. Series.
BS1235.2.G395 1999
222'.1106--dc21
                                                                99-28741
                                                                    CIP

First published in Great Britain by Lion Publishing plc, 1997.
First St. Martin's Griffin edition: January 2000.
10 9 8 7 6 5 4 3 2 1

Contents

ACKNOWLEDGMENTS

The Introduction has been taken from *Reading the Old Testament: An Introduction* by Lawrence Boadt, copyright © 1984 by permission of Paulist Press.

The text of 'Genesis in Literature' has been selected from *A Dictionary of Biblical Tradition in English Literature*, edited by David Lyle Jeffrey, copyright © 1992 by permission of Wm B. Eerdmans Publishing Co.

The abridged text of Genesis has been taken from the Revised English Bible copyright © 1989 by permission of Oxford and Cambridge University Presses.

From 'A Masque of Mercy' from *The Poetry of Robert Frost*, edited by Edward Connery Lathem, Copyright © 1947 by Robert Frost. © 1975 by Lesley Frost Ballantine. © 1969 by Henry Holt and Co., LLC. Reprinted by permission of Henry Holt & Co., LLC.: page 30.

'Wrestling' from *A Stone Diary* by Pat Lowther. Copyright © Oxford University Press Canada 1977. Reprinted by permission of Oxford University Press Canada: page 98.

'The Abyss', copyright © 1963 by Beatrice Roethke, Administratrix of the Estate of Theodore Roethke. From *The Collected Poems of Theodore Roethke* by Theodore Roethke. Used by permission of Doubleday, a division of Random House, Inc.: page 31.

'Fern Hill' by Dylan Thomas, from *The Poems of Dylan Thomas*. Copyright © 1945 by The Trustees for the Copyrights of Dylan Thomas. Reprinted by permission of New Directions Publishing Corp. and David Higham Associates: page 28

'If I Were Tickled by the Rub of Love' and 'I See The Boys of Summer' by Dylan Thomas, from *The Poems of Dylan Thomas*. Copyright © 1939 by New Directions Publishing Corp. Reprinted by permission of New Directions Publishing Corp. and David Higham Associates: page 28.

Foreword

Genesis is a wonderful book, one of my personal favourites in all of literature.

It is also a book that can be hard for us to read today. We are used to rational theology, psychological realism, religious morality and individual heroes. Genesis offers us none of these. It is an epic saga, like the *Odyssey* – a quest for home, except that its scale is far larger, spanning an infinitely greater swathe of both space and time, and deals with no individual hero (unless that is God's role) but a heroic community.

This community travels all the time; away from Eden and the mists before time, out onto the waters of the flood, into history, up from Ur of the Chaldees, northwards across the desert and around the great fertile crescent, down the eastern fringes of the Mediterranean, south into Egypt, back again into what will become Palestine, through prosperity and famine, and back to Egypt again.

Within this framework there are some extraordinary mythic adventures: Adam and Eve, Noah's ark, the destruction of Sodom, Jacob's courtship of Rachel. There are some moments of human pathos as touching as tragedy: Abraham's apparently insane attempt to sacrifice his son, Joseph's monstrous swaggering before his big brothers, Hagar building her altar of thanksgiving out in the dangerous desert, Sarah naming her long-awaited child Isaac after God's laughter. There are incidents of spine-chilling villainy and sublime virtue. There are some highly comic episodes. It is all here.

If you read this book looking for moral guidance you can only be appalled: murder, deceit, treachery, violence, megalomania and worse dot its pages. Even God is not straightforwardly kind or sensible; the humans are, broadly speaking, deplorable, though fully human. But if you read Genesis looking for stories, adventures, 'human interest', you cannot but be thrilled.

And within all this there is a profound sense of purpose. The Hebrew people are commended in modern history for the invention of monotheism but, oddly, that is not what I find exciting about Genesis. I read it as an adventure that established something radically new – faith in a God who is not confined to place, to temple or altar, a God who travels with the people, wherever they go and whatever they do.

Perhaps this is why Genesis does not end, like the *Odyssey* does, with the great triumphant homecoming – that is held over until later in the Old Testament. Because the real climax, the true completion of the quest, is the realization that here they are, in exile *again*, as far from the Promised Land as they were at the beginning – but now finally secure in the knowledge that their God is with them even there, and will be for ever. That adventure is worth all the danger.

Genesis is unique: it is narrative, creative, imaginative, theology of an unparalleled order – bolder, huger, more courageous, more outrageous, and with more special effects, than anything written since. It is not surprising that it has proved such an enduring and influential book, providing the foundation for not one, but three, of the greatest religions the world has ever known.

Sara Maitland

INTRODUCTION

The Book of Genesis covers a vast amount of time, stretching from the beginning of the world down to about 1500BC. According to geologists, the earth is at least 4 billion years old, and some anthropologists believe that humans have been around at least 2 million of those years. The authors of Genesis did not know much about this long history, nor did they care. They wished to sketch instead a few highlights about human origins that had particular religious significance for Israel's view of life, and to record a few traditions about their own ancestors that would help them understand how they came to be a people and a nation. In fact, 80 per cent of Genesis is dedicated to the few founding patriarchs, Abraham, Isaac and Jacob, and only 20 per cent to the remaining story of creation and life through the first 2 million years.

We cannot speak of a true sense of national history in Israel until the time of the exodus. The events of liberation from Egypt and conquest of land, added to the unifying power of a new religious faith built around the covenant with Yahweh, created the Israel whose history is the subject of all subsequent biblical narrative. Anything earlier is a kind of pre-history, a collection of remembrances and theological reflections that help throw light on the meaning of the exodus. Genesis can be understood somewhat like a special background briefing that government officials often give to newspaper reporters before a big event. Israel understood that God had begun something big in the exodus, but they also knew that God did not just begin to act on a whim. He had been involved in the world and in their story from the beginning. To indicate this concretely, they gathered early tribal traditions about great ancestors around a special theme of *promise*. Genesis 12–50 represents Israel's attempt to show that Yahweh had guided their ancestors in a way of promise up to the events of the exodus.

Finally, in the days of King David's new world empire, it seemed important to prepare a preface that would place God's saving actions for Israel in the light of his care for the whole world. Thus Genesis 1–11 began to take shape, and although it has the first place in the

Bible, it is by no means the first part to be written. Rather it is the fruit of prolonged thought and reflection over several centuries. But it is the place to begin the biblical *story*. Its strong images and rich language explore the depths of human experience at its most mysterious – the awesome wonder of creation, the joys of life, the agony of sin, the fear of death, the terrible human capacity for evil, the existence of God and the questions about his patience and justice. In bold strokes it makes us understand what God's *salvation* meant to Israel.

The Primeval History

Genesis 1–11, or the Primeval History as it is often called, can be broken into several stages:

1. Two creation accounts (Genesis 1–2)
2. The fall of humanity into sin and punishment (Genesis 3–4)
3. The list of ancient heroes from Adam to Noah (Genesis 4:17 – 5:32)
4. The story of how giants were born due to sin (Genesis 6:1–4)
5. The flood as punishment of that sin (Genesis 6:5 – 9:29)
6. The new list of nations spread across the world (Genesis 10)
7. The sin of the tower of Babel (Genesis 11:1–9)
8. The list of patriarchs from Noah down to Abraham (Genesis 11:10–32)

Source critics have shown that this outline in turn belongs to two basic sources, the 'Yahwist' and the 'Priestly':

Yahwist (J)	*Priestly (P)*
	Creation of the world (Genesis 1)
Creation of humans (Genesis 2)	
Sin and loss of Eden (Genesis 3)	
The sin of Cain (Genesis 4)	
	First list of patriarchs (Genesis 5)
The giants (Genesis 6)	
A flood story (Genesis 6–9)	A flood story (Genesis 6–9)
Table of nations (Genesis 10)	
Tower of Babel (Genesis 11)	Second list of patriarchs (Genesis 11)
Story of Abraham	Story of Abraham

The older of the two is Yahwist or J,[1] who has joined together several old stories and rewritten them to fit his religious message about Yahweh. Thus the original primeval history contained only those stories that are in the first column. They reflect Israel's thinking in the 10th century when it had become large enough as a nation to face other countries and their beliefs. It became important to discuss why God had chosen Israel over the nations, and why pagan beliefs, which seemed so attractive, were not faithful to God's will. Such a time of national confrontation and rethinking came under the great new empire of David and Solomon.

Examination of the J outline above shows that the original primeval history spoke mostly about how humans acted towards God and God's patient response. The J creation begins with humanity; other creatures are made for human use. All is rooted in goodness, but very soon sin enters into the picture and challenges God's rule through disobedience. For the Yahwist, early human history is continually a *four-part* story of *sin*, God's warning *punishments*, divine *mercy*, and then further *sin*. When Adam and Eve sin, God punishes them but promises future hope. Cain kills Abel (evil spreads more deeply), but God spares Cain's life even as he punishes. Soon humans multiply their wickedness and wanton behaviour, even unnaturally as in the story of the giants, and God sends the flood, but he spares Noah and restores humanity. Despite the blessing to Noah and the great increase of nations seen in Genesis 10, the people again rebel in pride to challenge God's rule by building a tower to heaven. God punishes them by confusing human languages, but again gives promise for the future in choosing Abraham.

J's purpose in Genesis 1–11 is to underline how God remains *faithful* to his human race despite their hardness of heart and frequent rejection of him. The author has taken ancient stories of various types and used them to show how God gave us dominion and responsibility for the world, the freedom to act on our own, and the gifts to achieve happiness. But through pride and a rebellious spirit, we have rejected this important task because we would not be subordinate to God. The sin in the human heart has unleashed on the world an evergrowing round of murder, war, and hatred, robbed us of life, and brought frustration and pain to our labours. But over and over again, the

11

theme of God's mercy to a sinful world can be heard in the background. It finds its strongest expression in the great compassion of God to Noah, his one faithful servant in the midst of worldwide corruption, by sparing him from the flood. Thus for the Yahwist, a true perspective of faith always includes the promise of *blessing* for our fidelity to God even while we know and experience the effects of sin and evil in us and around us. The beautiful promise of Genesis 8:21-22 sums up this hope:

> Never again shall I put the earth under a curse because of mankind, however evil their inclination may be from their youth upwards, nor shall I ever again kill all living creatures, as I have just done. As long as the earth lasts, seedtime and harvest, cold and heat, summer and winter, day and night, they will never cease.

In contrast to J, the P source materials in Genesis 1-11 focus on a few crucial events: the creation of the world, the destruction of life by flood, the restoration of blessing to Noah, and the family history of Abraham. Because the P writers were also the final editors of Genesis, they simply took the earlier J preface and worked it into their outline.

But on another level, P works out a wider theology built around the *goodness* of God's creation. P adds no more stories of sin to those already found in J, but concentrates on moments of blessing. Creation is entirely good and it reaches its peak in the blessing God bestows on Adam and Eve in Genesis 1:28:

> Be fruitful and increase, fill the earth and subdue it, have dominion over the fish in the sea, the birds of the air, and every living thing that moves on the earth.

Much of the Priestly account shows definite signs of its origin with the priests and temple schools: (1) the account of creation in Genesis 1 has the refrains and solemn tones of a liturgical prayer, not unlike the singing of the *Exaltet* at the Easter vigil in Catholic worship; (2) it emphasizes blessings and sacrifices as part of religious ceremonies; (3) it maintains an interest in precise genealogy lists, a task of ancient temple scribes who kept the birth, marriage, and death records, as well as most business contracts and debts; (4) it stresses the covenant

12

that God makes with all humans at the time of Noah, and which is later extended in a special way to Abraham and his descendants, and finally to Moses and the whole people of Israel.

Is Genesis 1–11 myth or history?

The stories in Genesis 1–11 certainly disturb the modern historian. They have no particular 'facts' that can be located in a given moment, no eyewitness reports, and no direct connections to other events that are known. If taken literally, the dates they do offer cannot be reconciled with the findings of geology about the age of the earth, nor do the lifespans of people conform to the ages of ancient human remains studied by anthropologists. They are much more like 'model' stories of how things *should have been* at the beginning, and resemble the literary creations of other ancient peoples. In all of them the moment of creation was not like any subsequent period of time. In that time the gods spoke directly to people. To the ancient mind it was a golden age; it was primeval time before history began.

In ancient thought, such time was expressed by means of certain traditional themes or motifs that were different from everyday language and experience. This type of literature is known everywhere as *myth*. Myths are not all of one kind, nor do they only speak of creation. They also tell stories of the gods, or of legendary heroes of old, or of the origins of customs and ethnic groups.

The common themes and motifs used in myths are the symbols cherished by all ancient civilizations. These include creation in or near water, a fight among the gods for order in the universe, the defeat of chaos by a hero god, the making of humans from mud or other lowly material, and a death and rebirth of the hero god parallel to the annual winter and spring cycle of nature. They explore the basic contrasts of nature: sun and earth, light and darkness, water and drought, male and female, gods and human creatures.

Genesis 1–11 incorporates many such elements into its stories, and many of its individual incidents find parallels in the myths of other ancient Near Eastern peoples, especially the Canaanites, Babylonians and Egyptians. Clearly, the biblical tradition did not hesitate to make use of these literary forms. But this does not mean that the biblical 'myth' always has the same view of the world as the original pagan story. So we must be careful to distinguish our use of the word 'myth' on two levels.

On the first level, myth is story using traditional motifs and themes. It is not scientific or historical in outlook as we would expect; it is more like folktale, but it does convey how the Israelites saw the shape of the world – it was their 'science', so to speak. A very good example of this use of myth is the description of the Garden of Eden in Genesis 2.

On a second level, however, myth is a 'theological' explanation of our relation to the gods, and often refers to ancient beliefs of a polytheistic nature in which natural powers were manifestations of the divine, where the gods were symbols of fertility and bound to the seasonal pattern of rainy and dry seasons, where each year the gods must reassert their power over the forces of chaos that threaten the world. When myth is used in this sense, we must be more careful about calling the biblical stories myths, for the authors of Genesis consciously intended to refute and contradict such a view of religion by reworking the traditional stories to *remove* any idea that there is more than one God, that the world is subject to chaos, that God is callous or uncaring, or that superstitious sexual practices are needed to renew nature. By telling the story of Genesis 1–11 as they did, stressing Yahweh's freedom and power versus human refusal of responsibility, the Israelites *demythologized* the myths – they destroyed the heart of pagan belief and reinterpreted the real meaning of the world in light of the one God who had revealed himself as saviour and ruler to Moses.

The patriarchs

After relating its lessons from human origins, the Book of Genesis focuses quickly on the history of one family that lived in northern Mesopotamia. Genesis 11:27–32 gives the family tree for Abraham in such a way that his grandfather, father and brothers are all named after towns that flourished in that area near the old caravan city of Haran. This was a device among ancient writers called 'eponymous' writing, and it helped to fix for the reader or listener the exact roots of the hero. The *eponym* is the person from whom a tribe or nation gets its name. A fine biblical example occurs in Genesis 19:36–38:

> In this way both of Lot's daughters came to be pregnant by their father. The elder daughter bore a son and called him Moab; he was the ancestor of the present-day Moabites. The younger also bore a son, whom she called Ben-ammi; he was the ancestor of the present-day Ammonites.

The traditions in Genesis 12–50 dwell on four such heroic ancestors: twelve chapters on Abraham, two on Isaac, nine on Jacob, and ten on Joseph, although, most properly, Joseph should be understood as part of the history of Jacob.

The Story of Abraham (Genesis 12–25)

The person of Abraham emerges suddenly and dramatically from the long list of persons in Genesis 11 when God addresses him out of nowhere in Genesis 12:1, 'Leave your own country, your kin, and your father's house, and go to a country that I will show you.' This marks the start of a new development in God's plan. The world as a whole is no longer the stage of action, but one small corner of it. The biblical picture of Abraham is told as a *journey* – Abraham moves through Canaan, stopping at major places in the mountain country, Shechem, Hebron and Beer-sheba, moving down into the southern Negev desert area, travelling even to Egypt. He indeed appears with a large number of followers and many flocks and herds, and he occasionally does trade (Genesis 15:2), but we really learn very little about any business dealings or even about his relationships with his Canaanite neighbours. The entire story of Abraham is presented to us in a way that stresses two major themes: (1) God made a *promise* to Abraham which will control all the events narrated in the Pentateuch,[2] but which already begins to unfold in Abraham's own lifetime; (2) God *blessed* Abraham and made him his specially chosen friend because Abraham was faithful to God. This second theme is summed up in Genesis 15:6, 'Abraham put his faith in the Lord, who reckoned it to him as righteousness.' But biblical tradition does not make

15

Abraham a perfect person without any flaws. In chapters 12 and 20 he tries to save his own life by giving up his wife Sarah and thus risking the promise of a son. In chapter 16 he is uncertain enough to take a slave girl in order to gain a son. In chapter 17, he doubts the angel who tells him that Sarah will bear a child. But these are rare moments in a life that stands open to God's direction. For one thing, Abraham always worships Yahweh wherever he stops on his travels – at Bethel in chapter 12, at Hebron in chapter 13, at (Jeru)Salem in chapter 14. He always accepts God's command to move on, and frequently has face to face experiences of God (chapters 15, 17, 18). In a moment of great sorrow, he obeys God and sends off his son Ishmael to a new life in order to prevent any threat to Isaac (chapter 21).

In all things Abraham proves devoted to God's command. But the ultimate test comes when God seems to demand that Abraham sacrifice Isaac back to him in chapter 22. This is the high point of the Abraham story, and the authors maintain a high sense of drama and artistic skill in narrating the horrifying moment. Abraham is weighed down so greatly that he cannot bear to tell Isaac the truth, and Isaac in turn is so trusting in his father that he never suspects what is happening. The boy asks naturally curious questions, and the grieving Abraham can barely answer. He preserves the privacy of the terrible last moments by sending the servants off. Just when all seems lost, God stops his hand and provides an animal to sacrifice instead. This story often shocks modern readers. They wonder how God could ask a thing like that. Perhaps the biblical authors themselves believed that Abraham could never go through with the act. But they wanted to make a point for all later Israel. It was not uncommon in the ancient world for parents to sacrifice a child in times of great need or illness to try to appease the gods. The Bible records several examples, ranging from Jephthah in the Book of Judges (chapter 11) down to Manasseh in the 7th century (2 Kings 21). All of these are looked upon with horror, and the story of Isaac certainly shows how Yahweh forbade any human sacrifice – he did not want human flesh but *would* accept animals as an offering instead, although he *most* wanted faith and trust.

This whole story sums up perfectly the character of Abraham as the man of faith. In Islamic traditions he is still called *khalil Allah*, 'the friend of God'. Even in the New Testament, St Paul cites Abraham as a model of faith in Romans 4:1–25 and in Galations 3:6–9. Abraham becomes the example for all Christians who believe in God's promise yet have never been part of the Jewish people.

The Story of Isaac and Jacob (Genesis 24–36)

After the purchase of a piece of the promised land by contract in chapter 23, the history of the patriarchs passes rapidly on to the stories of Isaac and Jacob. Isaac barely stands out in his own right, and serves mostly as a bridge to the saga of Jacob.

Basically, there are three different types of Jacob stories that were collected, probably separately from one another. *First*, there are a number of stories about the conflict between Esau and Jacob, who are said to represent Edom and Israel in the prophecy of Genesis 25:23:

> Two nations are in your womb and two peoples born of you shall be divided. One shall be stronger than the other; the elder shall serve the younger.

No doubt these stories were first cherished by Israel as *heroic tales* of their own superiority and greater cleverness compared with their neighbour and rival across the Dead Sea in Jordan, Edom.

Second, a group of *sagas* grew up around Jacob's marriages and his adventures with Laban, his Aramean relative. The tricks and deceits of Jacob and Laban against one another gave delight to Israelite audiences who saw in this single combat between heroes a mirror of the battle between the nation Israel and the Arameans in later days, in which Israel outfoxed Aram. Both the first and second group of stories, which pit Esau or Laban against Jacob, are really 'eponymous', where the individuals stand for the whole nations.

A *third* group preserved a number of *theophanies* of God to Jacob at various important shrines: Bethel in chapter 28, Mahanaim in chapter 32, Penuel in chapter 32, and twice at Bethel again in chapter 35. Israel treasured these traditions because they not only detailed God's blessing on special sites within their land, but they also provided a framework of divine guidance for Jacob, and special moments in which God reaffirmed his promise, made first to Abraham and renewed to Isaac in Genesis 26, and repeated now to Jacob.

In this collection of Jacob materials, the process of gathering the traditions together becomes easier to understand. We can trace the likely sequence of development from the oral state to the final written form. The three different types of stories were originally kept and transmitted for different reasons, sometimes by the same people, sometimes by others. The sagas of Jacob's conflict with Esau were *tribal stories* told about the times when the Jacob-tribe(s) first settled the land and had to fight for control. This 'history' was remembered in the form of the personal struggle between Jacob (Israel) and Esau (Edom), their chief rival for the land around the Dead Sea and the River Jordan. Single incidents may have been remembered by individual clans or villages but gradually were collected into a larger body of stories for the whole nation, probably in the period of the judges, between 1200 and 1000BC. The second group of stories about Laban and the Mesopotamian roots of the Jacob tribes began as *family histories*, but as relations between Israelites and Arameans turned into battles, these tales developed into hero sagas about how Israel bested the Arameans in their contests.

The divine appearances to Jacob may have originated in *local shrines*, where some divine appearance was remembered and drew worshippers to the holy place. At the time of the Hebrew conquest the Israelites associated the shrines near the areas that Jacob had lived with places where God had shown blessing and guidance to Jacob their ancestor.

The growth of so many traditions probably took centuries to become organized into an heroic epic that followed Jacob from birth to death. The crucial element that united them was the religious theme of God's choice and guidance, so that each incident and story could be fitted to the others as part of God's blessing. This stage, perhaps still completely oral, would have been achieved only after the exodus and conquest when the tribes would have developed a sense that they all belonged together as one people, and combined their individual traditions into one.

By the last editing under the Priestly school at the time of the exile in the 6th century BC, Genesis 12–36 had developed into a great epic of faith, including all the traditions from Abraham until the slavery in Egypt. But it still betrays its origins from the days when many of the stories were oral tales about the mighty exploits of a local leader over enemy tribes. Israel kept the whole tradition, warts and all, the way it had been passed down, because the people did not want to lose touch with their historical roots or with the way their ancestors remembered Yahweh, the God of history.

The Story of Joseph (Genesis 37–50)

The story of Jacob does not end in chapter 35. Although the following chapters, Genesis 37–48, focus on the person of one of his sons, Joseph, they remain only a sub-plot of the larger portrait of Jacob and his twelve sons. In concluding, Genesis 48–50 return to the final days of Jacob. There is also room for other additions along the way. Genesis 38 breaks the Joseph section with an incident about his brother Judah, and Genesis 49 is an ancient poem about the characteristics of the twelve brothers, who are the founders of the twelve tribes that make up Israel as a nation. Indeed, Jacob is important to the authors of Genesis because the twelve tribes came from him, but the action must shift in the story of Joseph to the rivalry between the brothers.

From one angle, the long story of Joseph is necessary in order to bring the tribes from the Palestine of the old days down into Egypt and into captivity in order to prepare for the exodus. The biblical writers must, in effect, set the stage for the next act. Yet the long Joseph narrative is remarkable for another reason. It makes a *single complete dramatic plot*, carefully woven together and leading to the moment when the brothers are reconciled with Joseph. It is far different from the short, independent sagas about the earlier patriarchs. Many modern biblical scholars refer to it as a 'novella', a short romantic novel. It delights in aspects completely ignored by the sagas: delighted descriptions of foreign customs, psychological insights, dramatic encounters, and detailed descriptions of Joseph's character – prudent, modest, gifted in dream analysis, well-spoken, and bred to nobility – in short, the perfect wise man of the world.

The plot is simple and yet a literary masterpiece. Joseph receives strange dreams in which he is more important than his brothers. This leads to their envy and Joseph finds himself in ever-deeper trouble. They sell him into slavery, he is falsely accused of adultery, and he ends in prison for life. Then with divine help the tide changes. He uses his dreams to help royal officials, then Pharaoh himself. He is made prime minister, and in the great famine that follows his brothers come into his power. But instead of doing to them what they had done to him, he forgives them and brings his father down to Egypt to live in peace and prosperity. The drama ends with the family reunited.

This is the kind of plot where nothing can be taken out as unnecessary. It is not just a collection of old incidents thrown together. But how did it become so different from the rest of the traditions in Genesis? The best solution understands that there must have been older saga stories about Joseph and about Israel's days in Egypt. But the Yahwist (or another) *rewrote* them into a novel about the time of Solomon, or even later, and it was included in the final form of the Book of Genesis.

There is some evidence for the early origin of many of the details. The coat of many colours (Genesis 37:3) was the type worn by early Semites pictured on the 18th-century BC tomb at Beni Hasan. The relations of the brothers are similar to tribal rivalries described in the Mari letters of the 18th century. The rise of a Semitic ruler to high position best fits the age of the Semitic Hyksos conquerors of Egypt in the 18th and 17th centuries BC. Various other incidents reflect a knowledge of Egyptian literature. Especially interesting is the similarity between Joseph's dealings with the wife of Potiphar and the *Tale of the Two Brothers*, in which the wife of the older brother tries to seduce the younger and when he resists, screams that he attacked her.[3] Another Egyptian tale tells of seven years of plenty followed by seven years of famine that matches the descriptions in Genesis 41.[4]

But the discovery of a statue in the city of Alalakh in Syria of King Idri-mi, who ruled about 1400BC, provides the most remarkable similarity of all.[5] The king inscribed on the statue how he quarrelled with his brothers, escaped to a foreign land where he was exiled for many years, received a series of oracles, gathered an army, reconquered Alalakh, became king, and forgave his brothers. It is not the same event historically, nor even the same plot, but it does share many themes in common with the Joseph story, and lets us see how the biblical tradition borrowed a number of well-known topics about the *reversal of fortune* and used them to show how God took care of Joseph. Joseph himself expresses this central message when he says to his brothers in Genesis 45:7–8:

> God sent me on ahead of you to ensure that you will have descendants on earth, and to preserve for you a host of survivors. It is clear that it was not you who sent me here, but God.

And again in Genesis 50:20 he says:

> You meant to do me harm; but God meant to bring good out of it by preserving the lives of many people, as we see today.

The Setting of the Patriarchal Stories

The lifetimes of the patriarchs are clearly set *before* the period in which Israel was in Egypt, and so can be dated no later than the 14th century BC. Although many elements in the tradition have been rewritten and updated over the centuries, the sources tried to preserve a description of the way people lived in the Middle Bronze Age, i.e. in the period from the 22nd century BC down to the 15th. Although a growing minority of archaeologists and biblical scholars think that much of the actual material in these chapters is fiction – in the sense that it is a romantic projection back from later times of an ideal life of faith – the majority still accept that there are genuine *remembrances* of this early period that form the *core* of the tradition. Many of the details about travel, semi-nomadic life, marriage customs and inheritance rights that are supposed in the narratives were well known in this period. The archives of Mari, a town on the Euphrates River in the 18th century BC, present several descriptions of nomadic life similar to that in Genesis 12–50. The archives of Nuzi, a town in northern

Mesopotamia in the 14th century, also present some close (but not exact!) parallels to customs mentioned in Genesis. The oral will of Isaac on his deathbed in Genesis 27:2 was also an acceptable legal practice in Nuzi, Esau's sale of his birthright (Genesis 25:31–33) is paralleled in a Nuzi contract, and the protected position of a slave woman who bears her master a son in place of a barren wife (Genesis 16) is known at both Nuzi and in the famous law code of Hammurabi (1700BC).

There is evidence also of a strong westward movement of Semitic peoples from Mesopotamia about 2100BC or earlier. These were known as Amorites ('Westerners'), and even if Abraham is not placed among them, it indicates the likelihood that such travels as his were normal. There is some mixed archaeological evidence that the Negev desert, which is the scene of much of the Abraham and Isaac tradition, was settled in the era around 2000BC, but largely deserted in the centuries after. A good case could be made for a period of prosperity there between 2000 and 1800BC under the secure rule of the strong pharaohs of the Middle Kingdom in Egypt. Trade and travel such as reported in Genesis 12:9 or 20:1 would be encouraged by such periods of stability. Moreover, the Bible itself remembers that Israel spent almost 400 years in Egypt between the arrival of Jacob and the time of the exodus (Genesis 15:13; Exodus 12:40). This would place Abraham even earlier, near the beginning of the second millennium.

The general description of the lifestyles of Abraham, Isaac and Jacob suggests that they were the chiefs of wealthy clans whose livelihood depended mostly on raising small livestock such as sheep and goats. They seem to have had semi-permanent roots near some large city, or at least within a definite area, but often moved with their flocks to new pastures according to the seasons of the year. Their life was not that of the city-dweller or villager, but they were never far from the major urban centres. Abraham settled near Hebron in the south, Isaac had connections to Beer-sheba in the same area, while Jacob dwelt in the area of Shechem and Bethel in the middle of Palestine. Among all the traditions, Abraham most appears to follow a semi-nomadic lifestyle, while Jacob seems the most settled. The story of how Joseph's brothers sold him to a caravan while they were pasturing their father's flocks far from home in Genesis 37 vividly illustrates this way of life. In good years, and in the mild winters, the clan stayed near the permanent settlement, but in the dry summer season or in years of drought, they might wander far abroad in search of grazing land and food.

The same incident in Genesis 37 hints at still another possible aspect of their life: *commerce* and *trade*. Their wide-ranging knowledge of the land, the safety of numbers in travel, and the likelihood that the clan had more members than herding required all support the suggestion that trade was an auxiliary part of their livelihood. Certain references to the longer journeys of Abraham especially make this an attractive idea. He moves between Haran, Damascus, Shechem, Hebron, and Egypt, all of which are on the caravan routes, all large cities or trading centres. A tomb painting from Beni Hasan in Egypt during the 18th century BC shows a Semitic clan of tinkers, metalsmiths and sellers of antelope meat visiting a local Egyptian prince to offer their goods and services. It could easily have been Abraham or Isaac.

The patriarchal story opens in Mesopotamia and northern Syria, and throughout Genesis the clans maintain their ties back to their original homeland. Both Isaac and Jacob go back to marry wives from among their relatives in Haran. Also many of the customs and practices in the Abraham narratives have parallels in documents from the ruins of 14th and 15th century Nuzi in upper Mesopotamia. This, too, is no doubt part of the original memory of Israel's ancestors.

Lawrence Boadt

Notes

1. The 'J' instead of a 'Y' comes from the German word 'Jahve', for it was German scholars who first proposed the abbreviations.
2. The first five books of the Bible (Genesis, Exodus, Leviticus, Numbers and Deuteronomy), traditionally referred to as the Five Books of Moses.
3. *Ancient Near Eastern Texts* 23–25.
4. *Ancient Near Eastern Texts* 31.
5. *Ancient Near Eastern Texts* 557–58.

GENESIS IN LITERATURE

Themes and Images

Apple

The 'apple' of the Old Testament is said to be fairest among trees, a good shade tree, bearing fruit of sweet savour (Song of Solomon 2:3) and pleasant odour (Song of Solomon 7:8). Of particular interest is the attribution of curative powers to the apple (still prevalent in the Near East), especially for sickness of heart or love-longing – 'Stay me with flagons, comfort me with apples; for I am sick of love' (Song of Solomon 2:5).

The association of the apple with love and lovesickness in the Song of Solomon seems early to have led to the identification of the apple with sexual temptation, and thus with the 'forbidden fruit' of the tree of the knowledge of good and evil – an association not made in the texts nor supported by modern biblical scholarship, but firmly entrenched by the confusion of the Vulgate *malum* (apple) with *malum* (evil), and reinforced by the designation of the deceptive fruit said to grow near the Dead Sea (Wisdom of Solomon 10:7; Josephus, *Jewish War* 4.8.4) as the 'apples of Sodom'.

The Edenic apple occurs as an image of deceiving beauty in one of Shakespeare's sonnets to the Dark Lady ('How like Eve's apple doth thy beauty grow, / If thy sweet virtue answer not thy show' [93.13–14]), but other Shakespearean references are chiefly folkloric or proverbial, lacking any significant biblical associations.

In visual representations, the depiction of the forbidden fruit of Genesis as an apple had become all but standard by the late Middle Ages and early Renaissance; prominent examples are paintings by Lucas Cranach the Elder, Titian, Tintoretto, and Rubens. Notable literary elaborations of the image appear in Donne's 'Progresse of the Soule' (stanzas 8–16) and in *Paradise Lost*, where Satan boasts: 'Him by fraud I have seduc't / From his Creator, and the more to increase / Your wonder, with an Apple' (10.485–87) – although Milton generally avoids reference to the apocryphal identification of the fruit with the apple. In what is perhaps the best-known passage in Milton's prose, he refers to the intermixture of good and evil in the postlapsarian

26

world by alluding to the fateful apple: 'Good and evil we know in the field of this world grow up together almost inseparably... It was from out the rind of one apple tasted, that the knowledge of good and evil, as two twins cleaving together, leaped forth into the world' (*Areopagitica*).

Byron reflects Lucifer's perverse interpretation of the apple as the gift of reason (*Cain*, 2.364, 529, 614, 664; cf. Genesis 3:5); in *Don Juan*, he alludes, humorously, to Eve's transgression ('Since Eve ate apples, much depends on dinner' [13.99.8]), and the reversal of the Fall effected not by Christ but Newton who, in 'discovering' gravitation, proved himself the 'sole mortal who could grapple, / Since Adam, with a fall or with an apple' (10.1.2).

Blake, another revisionist of biblical imagery, describes, in 'A Poison Tree', the fruit of secretly nurtured wrath as 'an apple bright' – a more truly evil fruit than that of Eden. The poison apple, familiar in other contexts (e.g., the tale of Snow White), recurs as the fruit of the Tree of Mystery in book 7 of *The Four Zoas* (228–306); the Tree of Mystery appears also in *America* and *Jerusalem*, under the names Urizen's Tree and Albion's Tree.

The apple of Eden makes a number of appearances in Robert Browning's *The Ring and the Book* (3.169–73; 4.851–59; 7.761–66, 828–29; 9.448–52). There is also one clear allusion to Song of Solomon 2:5, conflated in this instance with the signification of archetypal temptation: 'lust of the flesh, lust of the eye' (2.446–52). In Browning's 'A Bean-Stripe: Also Apple-Eating', the apple appears as an emblem of the natural world and occasions consideration of whether a personal creator stands behind the forces of nature. Similar associations of the apple with the course of human life are strongly present in Frost's 'After Apple-Picking', but in much modern usage the peculiar force of the biblical archetype has largely dissipated. Thus, the image is generalized, if prominent, in Yeat's poetry, both as the forbidden fruit (the 'brigand apple' in 'Solomon and the Witch') and as an emblem of love ('Baile and Aillinn' and 'The Song of the Wandering Aengus', in the latter of which the Master of Love pursues 'a glimmering girl / With apple blossom in her hair' and longs to 'pluck till time and times are done / The silver apples of the moon, / The golden apples of the sun' [17–24]).

In the poetry of Dylan Thomas, apples are emblematic of the libidinous energy of youth, often innocent, as in the opening lines of 'Fern Hill': 'Now as I was young and easy under the apple boughs / About the lilting house and happy as the grass was green... / And honoured among wagons I was prince of the apple towns.' In 'If I Were Tickled', the poetic persona imagines the fearless pleasure of erotic awakening: 'If I were tickled with the rub of love... / I would not fear the apple nor the flood / Nor the bad blood of spring.' Elsewhere, however, the poet contemplates 'the boys of summer in their ruin', carelessly 'setting no store by harvest', and sees how they 'drown the cargoed apples in their tides' ('I See the Boys of Summer'). More traditional yet is the imagery of 'Incarnate Devil', where the youthful sexuality symbolized by the apple is seen, by less innocent eyes, to be a 'shape of sin'.

George L. Scheper
Essex Community College
and John Hopkins University School of Continuing Education

Babel

Babel corresponds to Akkadian *Babili/u*, 'gate of the god(s)', but Genesis 11:9 explains it by a popular etymology with the Hebrew verb *balal*, 'to confuse'. The origin of the name itself, neither Sumerian nor Akkadian, is unknown. The tower is sometimes identified with the great temple of Nabu in the city of Borsippa, now called Birs Nimrud (corruption of Birj Nimrud, 'tower of Nimrod'), following early conflations with Nimrod, the descendant of Ham, whose kingdom is said to be Babel in Genesis 10:8–10. Penultimate among the 'primeval' narratives in Genesis, the Tower of Babel nonetheless marks the end of a road upon which humankind sets out after Eden, eastward before the watchful angel with its flaming sword.

The development of the tower narrative in English literature is erratic but colourful. It is altogether absent from the cycle plays, presumably because of its lack of liturgical import. Nimrod, however, is one of the imprisoned proud tyrants in Spenser's *Faerie Queene* (1.5.48.1; cf. Dante, *Inferno*, 31.77). John Donne has one clichéd reference to Nimrod's vain presumption in 'The Second Anniversary' (417). But with an eye on the language motif he creates an eerily brilliant character, his Mephistophelian accuser of 'Satire 4' who 'speaks all tongues' yet 'one language', insinuating: 'Nay, your apostles were / pretty linguists, and so Panurge was…'. Following this reference to Rabelais' Babylonian mischief (*Works*, 2.9), the strange petitioner

> … such wonders told
> That I was fain to say, 'If you had lived, Sir,
> Time enough to have been an interpreter
> To Babel's bricklayers, sure the Tower had stood.'
> (26–29; 58–59; 62–65)

For Herbert, on the other hand, Babel recollects the old adversity of invention and creation, inviting penance for a shared folly ('Sin's Round').

Milton's Nimrod (*Paradise Lost*, 12.24–62) is a subverter of 'fair equality, fraternal state', who arrogates 'dominion undeserved over his brethren' – a hunter not of beasts but of people who refuse his domination. His tower, built at the 'mouth of Hell' as a monument of fame, becomes an object of divine ridicule, aptly reduced to 'Confusion'. For Dryden, Babel images the schismatic dissenting churches (*The Hind and the Panther*, 2.470); in Swift's poetry it suggests confusion in politics and the state – 'Confounded in that Babel of the Pit' ('To Congreve', 122; cf. 'V's House', 66; 'Death of Dr Swift', 384). William Cowper's view of the calamity in *The Task*, by contrast, is, like Herbert's, sympathetic and imaginative of grace:

> When Babel was confounded, and the great
> Confed'racy of projectors wild and fain
> Was split into a diversity of tongues,
> Then, as a shepherd separates his flock,
> God drave asunder…
> Ample was the boon
> He gave them, in its distribution fair
> And equal. (5.193–200)

He notes that the peace did not last, and that the tradition of Cain and Tubal-cain, 'first artificers of death', was to continue in invention and war (208–229).

Blake's Vala, in crucifixion imagery drawn from Psalm 22, describes being let down from the gates of Jerusalem (Jerusalem, 1.22.2–8) by Nimrod, 'Jehovah's hunter'. This arresting inversion finds analogues in the Romantics. The Byronic hero can shout, 'Well done, old Babel! Ha, right nobly battled!' ('Deformed', 2.266; cf. 2.81; 1.677), and Byron himself fancies Nimrod as a romantic lover (Don Juan, 13.78). Keats' Otho will feast 'nobly as Nimrod's masons' (2.1.132).

Wordsworth, typically, is more traditional: 'Go back to antique ages' makes of the Tower of Babel what Chaucer did of Nimrod in his 'Former Age'; in the Prelude, the young French Republic, 'how Babel-like their task... by the recent deluge stupefied', promises its citizens 'to build a tower / For their own safety' (11.35–40). Elizabeth Browning makes a sentimental allusion to the notion of Babel as a painful separation of friends ('Victoire', 5; cf. Aurora Leigh, 5.554), while her husband forges an almost despairing resignation in his tragedy The Return of the Druses: 'All great works in this world spring from the ruins / Of greater projects – ever, on our earth, / Babels men block out, Babylons they build' (4.128–30).

In American literature of the period Melville's remembrance is merely cynical (Piazza Tales, 253), but Hawthorne is more subtly ironic when, in The Marble Faun, Miriam at the palace of the Virgin's Shrine in Rome begins 'to mount flight after flight of a staircase, which, for the loftiness of its aspiration, was worthy to be Jacob's ladder or, at all events, the staircase of the Tower of Babel'. Anna Hempstead Branch's Nimrod (1910) is a narrative poem based on the rebellion of Nimrod and his building of the tower in defiance of God.

James Joyce offers in Finnegans Wake 'a tour of Bibel', the pun proposing an alternative scripture even as it invokes the tower. But Robert Frost's less certain Jonah will later imagine an appropriate destruction for unrepentant New York:

> Babel: everyone developing
> A language of his own to write his book in,
> And one to cap the climax by combining
> All language in a one-man tongue confusion.
> (Masque of Mercy, 620.13–16)

This sobriety, at once reflective and prophetic, quietly anticipates Orwell's *1984* as well as C.S. Lewis' coven of scientists at the fortress of Belbury, where 'Babble about the *élan vital* and flirtations with panpsychism were... dragging up from its shallow and unquiet grave the old dream of Man as a God' (*That Hideous Strength*, chapter 9). Tolkien's dark towers, Minas Morgul and Orthanc, in *The Two Towers* echo a post-World War II uneasiness over the spectre of technology unhinged from ethics which, for Tolkien, has also its linguistic dimension in the fragmentation and diminishment of poetic 'elven' language. While the emphasis on pride and social fragmentation continues to be reflected in Morris West's *Tower of Babel* and William Golding's *The Spire*, it may be that the most profound echoes of Babel in the modern literary imagination, whether in nostalgia or apprehension about the future, have to do with a sense of diminished power of the word. Theodore Roethke puts an old question in contemporary accents:

> Among us, who is holy?
> What speech abides?...
> For the world invades me again,
> And once more the tongues begin babbling.
> ('Abyss', 2.8–9, 14–15)

David L. Jeffrey
University of Ottawa

Birthright

When Jacob wrested the birthright from his elder brother Esau by means of trading it for a mess of red pottage, Esau was relinquishing his spiritual inheritance, the covenant God had made with their grandfather Abraham (Genesis 12:1–8; 13:14–17).

Being the firstborn male in a Near Eastern society entitled one to numerous privileges, including a double portion of the material inheritance of the father (Deuteronomy 21:15–17). Substitution of a younger son for the eldest, thus overturning the order of primogeniture, is a significant theme in the Bible, affecting not only the stories of Jacob and Esau – repeated later in Jacob's 'adopting' of the two sons of favoured Joseph and the 'blessing' of the younger of these, Ephraim (Genesis 21:11; 48:5–19) – but also the story of David who, though the youngest son of Jesse, was made king, and of his own youngest son Solomon, who became king after him (1 Samuel 16:12; 1 Kings 1:28–30; 1 Chronicles 21:3; cf. Genesis 37:3; 44:20). Later, talmudic law provided for the disposal of property prior to death in accordance with parental preference, rather than strict adherence to the law of primogeniture (Hebrew *bekorah*; cf. the precedents usually cited, Genesis 21:10; Deuteronomy 21:15ff.). In the New Testament one of Jesus' most memorable parables concerns the relationship between the firstborn son and his younger brother, the latter of whom squanders his inheritance yet is 'favoured' by his forgiving father over the elder son, who in some measure 'despises' his own birthright by taking it for granted (Luke 15:11–32).

Renaissance authors found a classical analogue to the biblical tale of usurped birthright in the story of Titan and Saturn, one invoked by Spenser in his 'Mutability' Canto 6, and by Milton in the first book of *Paradise Lost*, where the classical and biblical contexts are in effect interwoven (510–13ff.). In book 3, God the Father tells Christ that while Adam's 'crime makes guilty all his Sons, thy merit / Imputed shall absolve them who renounce / Thir own both righteous and unrighteous deeds', adding that he 'has been found / By Merit more than Birthright Son of God' (290–92; 308–309). Donne makes a cosmological application in 'The Storm', where 'Darkness, light's elder brother, his birthright / Claims o'er this world, and to heaven hath chased light' (67–68). Robert Herrick takes up a New Testament reading in 'Coheires':

> We are Coheires with *Christ*, nor shall his own
> *Heire-ship* be lesse, by our adoption:
> The number here of Heires, shall be from the state
> Of His great *Birth-right* nothing derogate.

Crashaw contrasts two world-orders when he welcomes the infant Jesus 'to more than *Caesar's* Birthright' ('Hymn on the Holy Nativity'). Swift offers a parody of the Jacob and Esau exchange in 'Robin and Harry' (29–36), in which:

Robin, who ne'er his mind could fix
To live without a coach and six,
To patch his broken fortunes, found
A mistress worth five thousand pound;
Swears he could get her in an hour,
If Gaffer Harry would endow her;
And sell, to pacify his wrath,
A birth-right for a mess of broth.

The 'birthright' recognized by some Romantic poets is a kind of original pastoral harmony with nature. Wordsworth is the chief among nostalgic celebrants of this lost inheritance: 'With our pastures about us we could not be sad, / ... But the comfort, the blessings, and wealth that we had, / We slighted them all – and our birth-right was lost' ('Repentance', 21–24). An allusion to Esau's folly is muted in 'Vaudracour and Julia' (102–106; cf. 'Liberty', 21–26; 'Desultory Stanzas', 591–92). The theme is more extensively developed by Wordsworth in *The Prelude* (2.265–72; 10.209–221) and *The Excursion* (5.615–20; 8.276–82; 9.93–101). Ironic or parodic references to the mess of pottage are found in Byron's *Don Juan* (e.g., 5.351–52) and 'The Age of Bronze' (628–35), in which the predicament is cast in more modern terms:

And will they not repay the treasures lent?
No: down with every thing, and up with rent!
Their good, ill, health, wealth, joy, or discontent,
Being, end, aim, religion – rent, rent, rent!
Thou sold'st thy birthright, Esau! for a mess;
Thou shouldst have gotten more, or eaten less;
Now thou hast swill'd thy pottage, thy demands
Are idle; Israel says the bargain stands.

In Browning's 'Fifine at the Fair' a dilemma of the Prince is imagined as his being forced to 'sell... / His birthright for a mess of pottage' (520–31); the birthright characterized in 'Fillipo Baldinucci on the Privilege of Burial' (14.105–112) is akin to Wordsworth's (cf. 'Halbert and Hob', 1–4). In Browning's 'The Flight of the Duchess', his 'Smooth Jacob still robs homely Esau: / Now up, now down, the world's one see-saw' (907–908); as in Elizabeth Browning's *Aurora Leigh* (8.777–83) the birthright is here universal entitlement to social justice.

In American literature the Romantic legacy takes its characteristic form in Thoreau, who, in his essay 'Life without Principle', declares his resistance to the common lot: 'If I should sell both my forenoons and afternoons to society, as most appear to do, I am sure that for me there would be nothing left worth living for. I trust that I shall never thus sell my birthright for a mess of pottage.' Hawthorne draws the analogy familiar from English romanticism between 'the story of the fall of man' and 'our lost birthright' in *The Marble Faun* (chapter 47). The 'Fire and the Hearth' narrative in Faulkner's *Go Down Moses* (1940) involves a sold-out birthright and recollects the Jacob and Esau story. In Ezra Pound's *Cantos* the 'birthright of every man here and at home' is once again a political right to social justice rather than a 'blessing' or spiritual inheritance (64.56–58; 66.164–70). Something of both senses seems to be intended by Salman Rushdie in *Midnight's Children* in which the recurrent position of the narrator is Esau-like: 'Once more exiled from my home, I was also exiled from the gift which was my truest birthright: the gift of the midnight children' (284). These echoes of Kipling as well as of biblical tradition (recorded also in the Koran) culminate in a burning question (430):

> Why did midnight's child betray the children of midnight and take me to my fate? For love of violence, and the legitimizing glitter of buttons on uniforms? For the sake of his ancient antipathy towards me? Or – I find this most plausible – in exchange for immunity from the penalties imposed on the rest of us… yes, that must be it; O birthright-denying war hero. O mess-of-pottage-corrupted rival…

David L. Jeffrey
University of Ottawa

Creation

The Old Testament creation narrative (Genesis 1–3) is today commonly thought to be composed of two traditions. Genesis 1:1 – 2:3, known as the 'priestly' account, describes a process extending over six days which transforms a dark watery chaos through the creation of light, then provides an overarching heaven, dry land producing vegetation, the constellations, living creatures, and finally humankind, both male and female, created in the image of God. On the seventh day, according to Genesis 2:1–3, having completed the work of creation, God rested.

Genesis 2:4–23, generally thought to derive from an older, 'Jahwistic' tradition, begins with the creation of man from dust and the infused breath of life on the same (unspecified) day as the creation of heaven and earth – but before vegetation and animal life were made. God then planted a garden in Eden watered by four rivers, placed Adam in it, made animals for Adam to name, and finally made woman as Adam's companion out of a rib taken from him in sleep.

The two accounts can be regarded as complementary – the one establishing humankind's place in the scale of nature, the other his social role in a divinely arranged environment.

The creative power of God witnessed to in the book of nature is often celebrated in the Old Testament (e.g., Psalms 8:3; 19:1–3; 24:2; Jeremiah 27:3) and linked with the divine shaping of history (Isaiah 43:7, 15, 21; 44:2, 21, 24) and the divine wisdom (Psalm 104:24; Jeremiah 10:12). The New Testament stresses that creation was through the Son or Word of God (John 1:3; Colossians 1:15–18; Hebrews 1:2; 11:3) and links fallen humanity's hope for a renewed, transformed creation (Isaiah 65:17; 66:22) with the prospect of Christian redemption (Romans 8:19–25; 2 Corinthians 5:17).

Platonism rather than the Bible underlies most incidental literary allusions to creation. Human love appears repeatedly in Donne as analogous to the divine love which creates and upholds the world (e.g., 'The Canonization', 'Song: Sweetest Love I do not go', 'The Good Morrow'), but in the most extended treatment ('Nocturnal upon St Lucy's Day') the analogy is inverted: if love gives form and vitality to existence, its withdrawal allows a collapse into chaos and death (cf. Jeremiah 4:23–27), as the world will collapse at the end of divinely appointed time, a return to the 'Elixir' or the 'first nothing' from which creation stemmed. Rochester's later poem 'Upon Nothing' wittily develops this idea: if the divine creator had no antagonist from eternity, did Nothing exist, and if so, was it then Something? The round zero of nothing from which divine creation officially originated becomes a salacious and ironic image for the physical, sexual source of life created through love or lust, life which like the divine creation will at last return to nothing.

In the Renaissance it was asserted that poetic art also is analogous to the divine act of creation. Ben Jonson mingles creative love and creative art when he calls his dead son his 'best piece of poetrie' ('On my first Sonne', 9), and Marvell in 'The Garden' speaks of the mind's creations. Sidney's *Apology for Poetry* treats extensively the Neoplatonic concept of the brazen world of created reality opposed to the golden world created in art. In parts of *Arcadia*, giving a new twist to the long-standing fusion of classical pastoral and Golden Age poetry and the Christian paradise, Sidney attempts to follow out his own precepts about the moral force of re-creating in detail an exemplary pristine world of ideal innocence. The world of art and the actual, human world may both dissolve into nothing, however, as Shakespeare's Prospero reminds us: 'We are such stuff / As dreams are made on' (*Tempest*, 4.1.156–57). Human art is more kindly treated when Perdita and Polixenes agree that 'great creating nature' may be improved by a human art which is itself created by nature (*Winter's Tale*, 4.4.86–97). Much later the Romantics deliberately mingled poetic perception and creativity with the natural creation so that for Wordsworth nature is both what the senses 'half create / And what perceive' ('Tintern Abbey', 106–107) and Shelley laments a departed Keats as now 'a portion of the loveliness / Which once he made more lovely' ('Adonaïs', 388–89).

It was a traditional belief, stemming from God's observation that what he created was good (e.g., Genesis 1:4, 12), that at creation each created thing had its appointed nature and purpose and that noxious beasts and herbs became so only after the Fall (e.g., St Basil, *Hexameron*, 5.6; Luther, *Table Talk*, translated by T. G. Tappert (1967), 316). For Renaissance authors this meant that creation was a perfect work of art: according to Sir Thomas Browne creatures at worst were grotesques but not deformed, for nature was the art of God and there was beauty in the works of God 'being created in those outward forms which best express the actions of their inward forms' in the approved

Platonist manner (*Religio Medici*, 1.15–16). In the later Renaissance, metaphysical poets such as Marvell ('Upon Appleton House'), Vaughan ('The Recluse'), and Herbert ('Decay') pointed to traces of the divine creator in the natural world, faint glimmerings of the original message of the goodness and glory of the creator first written large in creation.

The work of creation as the inauguration of world history attracted both theological and historical discussion. Influenced by Plato's view that time itself was created with the world (*Timaeus*, 37d, e), Philo (*Legum allegoriae*, 1.2.2), St Hilary (*De Trinitate*, 12.40), and Augustine (*De Genesi ad litteram*, 4.33) suggest simultaneous creation of the world to be apprehended as taking place over six days so that God's complex work can be properly understood, a view reflected in Raphael's description of creation in *Paradise Lost*, book 7, and accepted by the Platonist Thomas Browne (*Religio Medici*, 1.45), though rejected by more biblicist commentators such as Luther (*Lectures on Genesis 1–5*, 1.4).

The divine creation as historical event is assumed by early universal historians (Eusebius, *Historia ecclesiastica* 1.2; Orosius, *History*, 1.3). Later, in the Renaissance, the indivisibility of history, theology, and natural science leads Sir Walter Raleigh (*History of the World*, 1614) to begin with the creation, influentially dated by James Ussher as commencing at night on 22 October 4004BC (*Annals of Creation*, translation 1662, 1). At the end of *Paradise Lost* human history has just begun and for Adam and Eve 'the world was all before them' (12.646). Creation associated with human history is central to Spenser's *Faerie Queene*, especially book 1: Archimago makes the false Una in parody of the Old Testament creation of Eve (1.1.45) and Redcrosse has a vision of the New Jerusalem (1.10.57), representing the other end of history. Una herself, good, beautiful, and true, the bride of Christ, represents an ideal of creation in the divine image such as the world has never seen since Adam fell, alluding to the New Testament vision of redeemed creation (cf. Romans 8:19–25).

The eclipse of traditional literal and historical readings of the biblical creation accounts can be linked with a gradual discrediting of so-called 'natural religion' after Hume's *Dialogues concerning Natural Religion* (1779). The majestic order of creation in the Old Testament, emphasized in Longinus' ascription of sublimity to the *fiat lux* of Genesis 1:2 (*On the Sublime*, 9.9) and in Calvin's account of God's wonderful power in ordering and sustaining the universe (*Institutes* 1.14.21), fostered a traditional belief in nature as the book of God, 'the Scripture and Theology of the Heathens' (Browne, *Religio Medici*, 1.16). Addison's ode 'The Spacious Firmament on High' (*Spectator*, 465, 23 August 1712) is an expansion of Psalm 19:1–3 arguing that the glories of creation demonstrate the existence of a creator, a view he attributes to Aristotle, though it is also Augustinian (*De civitate Dei* 11.6). This rationalist perspective leads Pope to link Newtonian science with the language of Genesis 1:2: 'Nature and Nature's law lay veiled in night: / God said: Let Newton be, and all was light!' ('Epitaph. Intended for Sir Isaac Newton') and to describe the spread of dullness in the *Dunciad* (4.652–56) as a return to primal chaos, an undoing of the divine creation embodying light and reason. William Paley's equation of creation with a watch bespeaking a watchmaker God (*Natural Theology*, 1802) sums up this tradition, but already Blake, reacting against Newton and 18th-century rationalism, had identified it with tyranny and limitation, and in his *First Book of Urizen* (recalling 'The first book of Moses', a subtitle of Genesis) he describes enslaved humanity as reversing the expanding creation: 'Six days they shrunk up from existence' (486).

The historicity of the biblical creation and Ussher's date of 4004BC were increasingly challenged in the 19th century in the face of geological evidence of the earth's immense antiquity and gradual formation and the associated development of evolutionary biology, a conflict described in retrospect in Edmund Gosse's autobiographical *Father and Son* (1907). Charles Kingsley's *Water Babies* contains an attempt to reconcile evolutionary theory with Christian beliefs. The new interest in scientific rather than divine origins was accompanied by a nightmare vision of the ultimate fate of the creation: Kelvin's second law of thermodynamics seemed to imply a cooling sun and chilly annihilation, a prospect entertained in Conrad's *Heart of Darkness* (1902) and visualized at the end of H.G. Wells' *The Time Machine* (1895).

Post-Darwinian theologians such as Karl Barth and Emil Brunner have stressed the moral and theological rather than historical dimensions of creation, and from the Romantics onward imaginative writers have developed ahistorical readings of the creation idea. In *The Four Zoas* Blake fused ideas of creation and fall in a myth of humanity created in a state of division but with the possibility of wholeness. Characteristically these later literary treatments involve adaptation of heretical sources or doctrines. The doctrine of the distinctiveness of God from his creation, regularly affirmed against emanationist or pantheist theories (see, e.g., Lactantius, *Divinae institutiones*, 3.28), was emphasized by the First Vatican Council of 1870, but both Wordsworth's sense of 'something far more deeply interfused / Whose dwelling is the light of setting suns' ('Tintern Abbey', 96–97) and Shelley's quasi-divine power inhabiting the splendours of Mont Blanc indicate a pantheist tendency in the Romantic celebration of nature. For W.H. Carruths, 'Some call it evolution / And others call it God' (*Each in his Own Tongue and Other Poems*, 1908). A post-Christian regenerated creation is envisaged at the end of D.H. Lawrence's *The Rainbow*: God's symbol guaranteeing the continuity of divine creation (Genesis 9:15–17) is transformed into a portent of 'the world built up in a living fabric of Truth'. William Golding's *Pincher Martin*, which is structured upon the six days of creation, shows an anticreation attempted by a wholly self-centred spirit deifying itself. And the gnostic view of the Demiurge as the evil source of creation, with affinities to Blake's Urizen, appears again as the 'sporting God' of Beckett's *Unnameable*.

The godlike creative role of the artist and his involvement in his creation are proclaimed with a new defiance in Lawrence's 'I was the God and the Creation at once' ('New Heaven and Earth', *Complete Poems*, 1964, 257). To the same end the Jewish Cabala which had influenced Milton and the Cambridge Platonists is exploited by Joyce: Stephen Dedalus broods on physical and imaginative creation and alludes in *Ulysses* to the cabalistic Adam Kadmon, an emanation of the creator God and himself a creator of worlds to come, a type of the artist for Joyce and for the boastful H.C. Earwicker in *Finnegans Wake*. More diffidently Wallace Stevens proposes the linguistic structures of the imagination as necessary fictions which create afresh the mental world which is our nearest approach to reality.

Brenda E. Richardson and Norman Vance
University of Sussex

Eden

The Hebrew word for Eden – possibly derived from Sumerian–Akkadian *edinu* ('plain, steppe') – refers to the location of a garden planted by God for the habitation of humanity (Genesis 2:8, 10; 4:16). The term comes by association also to indicate the garden itself (Genesis 2:15; 3:23–24; Ezekiel 36:35; Joel 2:3), which is elsewhere called the 'garden of God' (Ezekiel 28:13) or 'garden of the Lord' (Isaiah 51:3). The Septuagint and Vulgate translate the name from a homophonous Hebrew root (*adanim*) meaning 'delight' (i.e., Septuagint *paradeisos tes tryphes;* Vulgate *paradesus deliciarum* = 'paradise of delight' [Genesis 2:15]), leading to the traditional interpretation of the garden as paradise.

In English literature Eden is usually alluded to as a lost paradise (historical, mythic, or figurative). The traditional association of paradise with marital bliss is given ironic treatment in Chaucer's *Merchant's Tale* (e.g., 4.1264–65, 1331–32); the walled garden, with its deception, suggests an Edenic 'fall'. In Spenser's *Faerie Queene* the Redcrosse Knight seeks to protect Eden, a land of uncorrupted human nature, from the dragon Satan (1.10.46; 1.12.26). (A more ambiguous Spenserian garden, though with some Edenic qualities, is the 'Joyous Paradise' [3.6.29.1] of the Garden of Adonis [3.6.29–40].) One of the best-known false paradises in English literature – comparable to the Garden of Deduit in the *Romance of the Rose* – is Spenser's Bower of Bliss, which is compared ironically with Eden (*Faerie Queene* 3.13.52).

England is described as 'other Eden, demi-paradise' by the dying John of Gaunt in Shakespeare's *Richard II* (2.1.42); later in the same play, however, the prelapsarian image is undercut when England is likened to a weed-infested garden (3.3.55–57; similar images recur in the Henriad [e.g., *Henry IV* (2), 4.1.203ff.; 4.4.54–56; *Henry V*, 5.2.37ff.]). Andrew Marvell offers no such qualification in hailing Britain as 'Thou Paradise of the four seas' ('Upon Appleton House', 323). Dryden praises Charles II as the 'royal husbandman' who has rid his paradise of 'rank Geneva weeds' (*Threnodia Augustalis*, 354–63). For many, however, nostalgic longing for a pristine garden of new beginnings was redirected from England to the New World. Thus

Michael Drayton envisions Virginia as 'Earths onely paradise' ('To the Virginian Voyage', 23–24; cf. Marvell's 'Bermudas'), while Thomas Morton is typical of many colonists in finding New England 'Paradise... Natures Masterpeece' (*New England Canaan*, 1637; reprinted 1883, 180).

The most influential literary depiction of Eden in English is in Milton's *Paradise Lost*, which, while providing a rich examination of the psychological and spiritual habitation (it is a place of 'Truth, wisdom, and sanctitude' [4.293] and knowledge [8.272–73]), affords also an unprecedented wealth of elaborate descriptive detail frankly borrowed from classical texts:

> ... Thus was this place,
> A happy rural seat of various view:
> Groves whose rich Trees wept odorous Gums and Balm,
> Others whose fruit burnisht with Golden Rind
> Hung amiable, *Hesperian* Fables true,
> If true, here only, and of delicious taste:
> Betwixt them Lawns, or level Downs, and Flocks
> Grazing the tender herb, were interpos'd
> Of palmy hillock, or the flow'ry lap
> Of some irriguous Valley spread her store,
> Flow'rs of all hue, and without Thorn the Rose:
> Another side, umbrageous Grots and Caves
> Of cool recess, o'er which the mantling Vine
> Lays forth her purple Grape, and gently creeps
> Luxuriant; meanwhile murmuring waters fall
> Down the slope hills, disperst, or in a Lake,
> That to the fringed Bank with Myrtle crown'd,
> Her crystal mirror holds, unite thir streams.
> The Birds thir choir apply; airs, vernal airs,
> Breathing the smell of field and grove attune
> The trembling leaves, while Universal *Pan*
> Knit with the *Graces* and the *Hours* in dance
> Led on th' Eternal Spring... (*Patrologia Latina*, 4.246–68)

Milton's version of the Edenic landscape had a lasting impact on the popular imagination. The wealthy began to trim their estate gardens in 'miltonic' style because of its pleasing sublimity, and estate poetry, already popularized by Jonson, Carew and Marvell, became highly fashionable, with elevated, often spurious, comparisons being drawn between the horticultural details of the garden in question and that of the earthly paradise. Inscribed in one of the alcoves of the Welwyn garden of Edward Young was the phrase: *'Ambulantes in horto audiverunt vocem Dei'* – a mere stylish fancy, for as Alexander Pope, himself a master gardener, acknowledged: 'The Groves of Eden, vanished now so long, / Live in description, and look green in song' ('Windsor Forest').

In Blake's prophetic books, Eden is consistently a higher spiritual paradise, a realm of life, generation, and harmony, while Beulah, a lower paradise, is closer to the Garden of Genesis 2 (cf. especially *Milton*, section 30; *Jerusalem*, pl. 28; and *Descriptive Catalogue*, no. 578A). The natural world is seen as Edenic by Thomas Traherne (*Centuries*, 3.3), William Cowper ('Retirement', 28; *The Task*, 3:296–99), and pre-eminently by William Wordsworth, who in *The Prelude* (3.108–109) speaks of 'Earth nowhere unembellished by some trace / Of that first Paradise whence man was driven'. A similar perception occurs in *The Excursion* (9.714–19).

The self-conscious scepticism of the 19th and 20th centuries is frequently highlighted in literature. Shelley in *Queen Mab* refers to 'fabled Eden' (4.89), and Robert Browning's Sordello (4.304) and Mr Sludge (1431–32) disparage the 'Eden tale'. Emily Dickinson's whimsical wit toys with 'Eden – a legend dimly told' (no. 502; cf. nos. 215, 1545), while Matthew Arnold simply asserts 'the story is not true' (*Complete Prose Works*, 1960–77, 7.383). Satiric works set in Eden include Mark Twain's *Diary of Adam* and *Diary of Eve* and Act 1 of G.B. Shaw's *Back to Methuselah*.

Even in an age of scepticism, however, the Eden story has continuing power for such writers as George Eliot (e.g., chapter 49 of *Felix Holt*). It provides a mythological or symbolic framework for Charles Dickens' *Martin Chuzzlewit* (chapters 21, 23) and *Great Expectations* (chapter 19), Nathaniel Hawthorne's *The Marble Faun* (chapters 27, 31), William Faulkner's 'The Bear' (long version, section 4), and a predictable series of punning allusions in James Joyce's *Finnegans Wake*. In his space thriller *Perelandra*, C.S. Lewis re-creates an Edenic landscape, temptation, and fall on the planet Venus, inviting serious theological reflection on the biblical story.

David W. Baker
Ashland Theological Seminary
Joseph E. Duncan
University of Minnesota

East of Eden

When Cain was sent out as a perpetual fugitive he 'went out from the presence of the Lord, and dwelt in the land of Nod, on the east of Eden' (Genesis 4:16). Since 'Nod' in Hebrew means 'wandering' – an irony noted by St Jerome – there is a double edge to Cain's condemnation. He wanders in the land of wanderings. To 'drop into the Land of Nod' has come to mean to have wandering thoughts or daydreams, or to fall asleep; Melville's Ishmael uses the phrase in this way in *Moby Dick* to describe his nearly unfortunate nap in the Spouter Inn, and Charles Reade's narrator uses it of his 'lady' in this sense in *Hard Cash* (chapter 17). Talmudic lore assigns to the area east of Eden the abode of Adam also after the Fall (Konen 29), the view that paradise itself was in the east being based upon Genesis 1:8 (although some rabbinic authorities understood that there was a preexisting paradise situated in the west, or northwest [Berakot 55b; Ethiopic Enoch 32]). Early English literary references are typically to the monstrous or reprobate descendants of Cain, as in Sir Walter Raleigh's *The History of the World*, where the Henochii, citizens of Cain's city Enoch, are said to dwell 'towards the east side of Eden, where Cain dwelt'. Sir John Mandeville reflects the tradition that one of Noah's sons, Ham, inherited the east after the flood, seizing it by cruelty, and that his son was Nimrod the giant, who built the 'tower of Babylon'. The people of Ham were said to have sexual commerce with demons, producing monstrosities of all kinds, the ultimate incarnation of which was 'the Emperor' or Ghengis Khan, with his 'Lordes from the east' (*Travels*, chapter 24).

Dryden, in his essay 'Virgil and the Aeneid', calls Cain the first traveller, who 'went into the land of Nod' before either Ulysses or Aeneas was born. But the less pleasant associations with Cain persist, both whimsically – as in the case of O. Henry's loquacious interlocutor's wife in 'Municipal Report', who though she 'traced her descent back to Eve' felt it necessary to deny 'any possible rumour' that she may have had her beginnings 'in the land of Nod' – and sombrely, as in John Steinbeck's novel *East of Eden* (1952). In this dark and loosely biblical saga the protagonist Adam Trask marries and moves west to California with his twin sons Caleb and Aron, only to be abandoned there by his sinister wife, who becomes a brothel madam in Salinas after murdering its previous owner.

David L. Jeffrey
University of Ottawa

Fall

The Fall traditionally refers to the first human transgression of the divine command. The biblical narrative gives an account of this transgression, including the events leading up to it and its immediate consequences. Doctrinally the narrative is usually interpreted as describing the cause and nature of humanity's wickedness, suffering, and estrangement from God. In turn, the doctrine influences how the narrative is read or rewritten. But stories of the Fall and doctrines of the Fall are not necessarily interdependent, and should be distinguished.

The story of the Fall is told in Genesis 2–3: the Lord God, having created man (Adam), placed him in the Garden of Eden and commanded him not to eat of the tree of the knowledge of good and evil: 'for in the day that thou eatest thereof thou shalt surely die' (Genesis 2:17). After woman was created, the serpent spoke to her, contradicting God's warning about the consequences of eating the forbidden fruit and ascribing to God a jealous motive for his interdiction: 'God doth know that in the day ye eat thereof, then your eyes shall be opened, and ye shall be as gods' (Genesis 3:5). The woman then tasted the fruit and gave some to her husband, who likewise ate. Immediately they knew themselves to be naked (Genesis 3:7), and hid themselves. God responded to their transgression by pronouncing a threefold curse: the serpent will crawl on its belly and eat dust; the woman will experience sorrow in bearing children and be dominated by her husband; and the man will sorrow and sweat to obtain food from the ground (Genesis 3:14–19).

The rest of the Old Testament makes no clear mention of the story of Adam and Eve (but cf. Job 31:33; Ezekiel 28:12–15; see also 4 Ezra 3:5–8; 7:11–13). According to various apocrypha and pseudepigrapha, such as Slavonic Enoch, Satan (Sotona, or Satomail) attacks humanity by means of an actual seduction of Eve: 'He conceived thought against Adam, in such form he entered and seduced Eve, but did not touch Adam' (31:6). But the familiar biblical interpretation of the Fall is given in the New Testament by St Paul (Romans 5:12–21; 1 Corinthians 15:21–22), who treats the story as authoritative and archetypal. Paul focuses principally on the sin of Adam as being, in its nature and consequences, significant for the entire human race, and symmetrical with the sinlessness and life-giving acts of Jesus Christ, whom he calls 'the last Adam' (1 Corinthians 15:45): 'For since by man came death, by man came also the resurrection of the dead. For as in Adam all die, even so in Christ shall all be made alive' (1 Corinthians 15:21–22). Similarly in Romans, Paul declares, 'For as by one man's disobedience many were made sinners, so by the obedience of one shall many be made righteous' (5:19). In this way, he amplifies and universalizes the significance of Adam and of his transgression by making them the backdrop against which Christ's redeeming acts are to be read. (References such as 4 Ezra [2 Esdras] 3:5–8, 21 and 7:11–13 suggest that the idea that Adam's sin had universally baleful effects was held in ancient Jewish circles as well as in early Christianity.)

Typological interpretation also links the serpent in the Fall story to Satan himself. For if the second Adam was tempted by Satan (Mark 1:13), must it not also have been Satan who tempted the first Adam? In Revelation, John makes the identification explicit, referring to the overthrow of 'that old serpent, called the Devil, and Satan' (Revelation 12:9). The same identification is supported by the words of Jesus: 'I beheld Satan, as lightning, fall from heaven. Behold, I give unto you power to tread on serpents and scorpions, and over all the power of the enemy' (Luke 10:18–19; see also Romans 16:20).

The Bible nowhere uses the term *Fall* in connection with the story of Adam and Eve. Once the story is read as involving the agency of Satan, however, the first transgression of Adam is plausibly paralleled with the first transgression of Satan. The latter is suggestively described in terms of a 'fall from heaven' by Jesus in Luke 10, and traditional interpretation of Isaiah 14 sees the fall of the proud king of Babylon as post-figuring that of Satan: 'How art thou fallen from heaven, O Lucifer, son of the morning!... For thou hast said in thine heart, I will ascend into heaven... I will be like the most High. Yet thou shalt be brought down to hell' (14:12–15).

In English literature the Fall story is sometimes retold or treated thematically in analogues and echoes of that story, and doctrinally in literary interpretations of evil and of the human condition. Milton's *Paradise Lost*, which is the most influential treatment of the Fall in English, comprehends both the story of Adam and Eve and its main predecessor and analogue, the fall of Satan, and has much to say also about the condition of fallen humanity – 'death... and all our woe' (*Patrologia Latina*, 1.3). Milton combines maximizing and minimizing interpretations, emphasizing Adam and Eve's prelapsarian glories and the profound consequences of their sin, but also depicting the prelapsarian conditions for their further sinless growth and development, including work, storytelling, instruction, mutual deliberation and understanding, and what Milton refers to as 'the triall of vertue' (*Areopagitica*, 1644; in *Complete Prose Works*, 1953–82, 2.528).

Other notable English treatments of the Fall story are found in the Old English *Genesis B*, in the Middle English mystery plays, and in *Cursor Mundi*. Spenser's *Faerie Queene* (book 1) recounts how Una's parents, Adam and Eve, after long exclusion from their native land (Eden) by a dragon (Satan), are restored to it by the Redcrosse Knight (Holiness). Other notable Renaissance retellings, in addition to Milton's, include those of Du Bartas, Grotius, and Vondel. Sidney incorporates 'the accursed fall of Adam' into his poetics early in the *Apology*. Dryden's *The State of Innocence and Fall of Man* (1712), based on *Paradise Lost*, begins to blur, perhaps unintentionally, the distinction between pre- and postlapsarian existence. In *An Essay on Man*, Alexander Pope presents a naturalistic version of the prelapsarian 'state of Nature', which becomes undermined by a general outbreak of unenlightened self-love (3.147–282).

In America, Nathaniel Hawthorne memorably explores the nature of fallen humanity and the mystery of sin in *The Marble Faun* and *The House of the Seven Gables* and in his short stories 'Rappaccini's Daughter' and 'Young Goodman Brown'. Still other writers, such as Archibald MacLeish (*Songs for Eve*), revise the story altogether in order to portray the Fall as actually desirable for the evolution of human consciousness, a view with antecedents in 1st- and 2nd-century gnostic writings.

Such diverse poets as Thomas Traherne and William Wordsworth present pictures of the paradise of childhood followed by a 'fall' into adulthood (cf. Gerard Manley Hopkins' 'Spring and Fall', Dylan Thomas' 'Fern Hill', and E.E. Cummings' 'in Just spring').

Different writers use the Fall story for very different doctrinal ends. Godfrey Goodwin in *The Fall of Man* (1616) paints a pessimistic view of human nature and history based on a thoroughly maximizing view of the Fall; but George Hakewill, in *An Apologie for the Power and Providence of God* (1627), without at all rejecting the story of the Fall, opposes Goodwin's gloomy conclusions regarding its consequences by postulating a correspondingly high view of the grace and power of God in mitigating those consequences. Or, again, a writer like Thomas Hobbes, who does not use the Fall narrative at all, in fact creates his own etiological myth of the 'natural condition of mankind' against the backdrop of the orthodox Fall story and raises parallel questions concerning human nature, human misery, and the relief of human misery (see *Leviathan*, 1.13).

In thought and literature since the Romantic period, as suggested in the example of MacLeish, the tendency increasingly has been to revise both the story and the doctrine of the Fall. For centuries Christian interpreters have wondered whether the Fall, if it occasioned the advent and work of Christ, could ultimately be regretted; hence the paradoxical view of the 'felix culpa'. But Shelley openly assumed a view of the fall of Satan as Promethean and progressive (see the preface to *Prometheus Unbound*). What Shelley did for Satan, the evolutionism of the later 19th century did for humankind, so that 'Fall' was radically reinterpreted as 'progress'.

And yet modern literature by no means sustains an optimistic view of human nature or the trajectory of civilization. The story of the

Fall, what Terry Otten has called 'this most elemental of myths', thus appears 'woven into the texture' of modern literature (T. Otten, *After Innocence*, 1982, 7). It can be seen as either undergirding or background, e.g., in the fiction of William Golding (*The Inheritors, Free Fall, Lord of the Flies*), Joseph Conrad (*Heart of Darkness*), and Albert Camus (*La Chute*); in the fantasy of Lewis Carroll (*Alice in Wonderland, Through the Looking Glass*), C.S. Lewis (*Perelandra*), J.R.R. Tolkien (*Lord of the Rings*), and Stanley Kubrick and Arthur C. Clarke (*2001: A Space Odyssey*); and in the drama of Edward Albee (*Who's Afraid of Virginia Woolf?*). For even in its most basic form, in Genesis 2–3, the story of the Fall not only speaks of the first man and the first woman naked before each other and God, thus engaging the reader's sense of entanglement in the complex web of progenitor and progeny, of genesis and generation; it also faces the mystery of the perverse will that listens to the voice of the beast rather than the voice of God, and chooses death rather than life.

Dennis Danielson
University of British Columbia

Flood

Genesis 6–9 describes the flood by which God punished sinful humanity, sparing only Noah and his family, along with representatives of all the animals, in an ark constructed according to divine directions. The waters came from forty days of rain (Genesis 7:4, 12) heightened by primeval waters erupting from the 'fountains of the great deep' and pouring through 'the windows of heaven' (7:11).

The Genesis story resembles the flood narrative in the Gilgamesh epic and shares some characteristics with many other flood stories from all over the world. The Greek parallel, in which Jove punishes the evil world, sparing upright Deucalion and his wife, is found in Ovid's *Metamorphoses* and given English form in the late 17th century by Dryden in his translation (*The First Book of Ovid's Metamorphoses*, 193–606).

The basic structure of the Genesis version is simple: God decides to destroy his creation but to save some of his creatures; after the catastrophe he establishes a covenant with Noah, promises never again to send a flood, and thus makes life on earth possible again. In Isaiah 54:9 the Lord repeats his promise never to send another flood (Genesis 9:9–11). In the New Testament the flood and the ark are taken as examples of divine judgment and salvation (Matthew 24:37–39; 1 Peter 3:20–21; 2 Peter 2:5), and Noah as an example of faith in God (Hebrews 11:7).

In the 16th and much of the 17th century the flood story is treated in unremarkable ways, drawing on the biblical account and its commentaries for detail. Following the example of Du Bartas' *Divine Weekes*, some writers, including William Hunnis and Francis Sabie, retell the biblical narrative in verse. Michael Drayton, in *Noah's Flood*, is especially interested in the loading of the ark, the nature and consequences of the deluge, and the joy of the animals at the end of the flood. He takes up a number of controversial points and insists on the veracity of the story. So also does Milton in *Paradise Lost* (11.556–900). Skilfully alternating between Michael's account and Adam's reactions to it, he emphasizes the wickedness of the antediluvian generations, Adam's sorrow about the destruction of creation, and his joy concerning Noah for whose sake God raises another world.

In Shakespeare's *Comedy of Errors* (3.2.105–107) references to the flood and the apocalypse are combined in a witty dialogue between Dromio and Antipholus (cf. *As You Like It*, 5.4.35–38). In Donne's *The First Anniversary* the ark's dimensions are said to parallel the proportions of a human body and the vessel thus typifies the individual Christian (cf. 'To Sir Edward Herbert at Julyers'). In 'A Hymne to Christ' Donne adopts conventional baptism–salvation typology, which appears also in Crashaw's 'Upon the Bleeding Crucifix'. Herbert expresses grief in connection with the first return of Noah's dove ('The Church'). Elsewhere he identifies the ark with the Church ('Affliction') and speculates that the place where Noah landed was the starting point of Abraham's journey towards Egypt with the ark of the covenant ('The Church Militant'). Vaughan connects the ark with the pillar of Jacob's vision, the Temple, and the individual soul ('Jacob's Pillow and Pillar') and recalls God's covenant with Noah ('The Rainbow'). Marvell draws on traditional typology in

'Upon Appleton House', but in other instances provides a political application, associating Cromwell's son with the rainbow after the deluge ('A Poem upon the Death of His Late Highness the Lord Protector'). The Royalists employed a similar strategy. Dryden begins his poem 'To His Sacred Majesty' by comparing Charles' landing in England with Noah's on Mt Ararat, a reading perhaps influenced by R. Filmer's *Patriarcha*, which Locke attacked in 'An Essay Concerning False Principles'.

As the literal accuracy of the story began to be questioned more openly, satiric and trivial treatment of the flood in literature became increasingly common. Edward Ecclestone's drama *Noah's Flood* (circa 1679) toys with biblical material and Miltonic themes. Swift makes a series of satiric allusions in 'Ode to the Athenian Society', 'An Answer to Dr Delany's Fable of the Pheasant and the Lark', and 'A City Shower'. Hardy, in *Under the Greenwood Tree*, pokes fun at Mrs Day, who, when furnishing the house, follows the principle established by Noah of having two articles of every sort. In *Far from the Madding Crowd* he compares Oak's shepherd's hut and its environment to a small Noah's ark on a small Ararat.

For Wordsworth the story provides a backdrop for meditation on the natural world: the dove is the happiest bird of the ark ('A Morning Exercise') and a symbol of hope ('The Waggoner', 1.53). In his sonnet 'Sky-prospect' Wordsworth imagines seeing Ararat and the ark in the west, but then reassures himself that 'all is harmless' – the vista innocent of any hint of destruction.

For Carlyle, heroic man finds himself adrift and clutches at literature, 'wonderful Ark of the Deluge, where so much that is precious, nay priceless to mankind, floats carelessly onwards through the Chaos of distracted times'. Emerson, likewise, in 'The Poet' likens the poet's mind to a Noah's ark. In Tennyson's 'Two Voices' the pessimistic voice seems to wreck the poet's 'mortal ark', but then a hidden hope, like a rainbow, breaks out of the speaker's sullen heart (cf. *In Memoriam*, 12).

Byron alludes to the flood several times in *Don Juan*, and in *Childe Harold's Pilgrimage* (4.826–28) he associates the Napoleonic era with a universal deluge for which there is no ark. Like West, Turner, Danby, and Doré in their deluge paintings, Byron sides with the victims of the flood: his uncompleted play *Heaven and Earth* draws more on the apocryphal book of Enoch than Genesis, expanding references to a liaison between 'the sons of God and the daughters of men', which in the Bible is condemned as one of the evils which prompted God's wrath before the flood (Genesis 6:2–4; Ethiopic Enoch 6–9, 54–55): two angels fall in love with the daughters of Cain, and, rejecting God's warnings, escape with them from the earth, which is about to be deluged.

In James Thomson's 'The City of Dreadful Night' a preacher tells his melancholy brothers who are 'battling in black floods without an ark' that there is no God. George Eliot, in *The Mill on the Floss*, describes young Tom's dream of building a Noah's ark in case of a flood: ironically, years later Maggie tries in vain to save Tom and herself from drowning. Hardy shows God repenting, as in Noah's time, that he 'made Earth, and life, and man' ('By the Earth's Corpse') and satirizes the bourgeois who have learned to 'hold the flood a local scare' and on Sundays read Voltaire ('The Respectable Burgher on "The Higher Criticism"'). Kipling, in 'The Legend of Evil', is indebted to folk legends in suggesting that the salvation of Noah and his family was ineffective because the devil got into the ark when Noah cursed the stubborn donkey.

Melville was fascinated with the flood story, and the continuing impact of the flood is a central preoccupation of the characters in *Moby Dick*. Nantucketers' boats are said to be their arks. Ahab sees waters the same as Noah's; after Moby Dick's victory, 'the great shroud of the sea rolled on as it rolled five thousand years ago' in Noah's days. Ishmael remarks that 'Noah's flood is not yet subsided', but the sea in this instance is controlled by no mercy and no power but its own. Mark Twain describes what he perceives as the absurdity of the biblical story and comments bitterly on the victims of the deluge ('Adam's Soliloquy').

Modern scepticism concerning the narrative is summarized by Dickinson in 'The Winters Are So Short': 'But Ararat's a legend – now – / And no one credits Noah'. In his preface to *Back to Methuselah* G.B. Shaw asserts that 'The feeling against the Bible has become so strong at last that educated people… refuse to outrage their intellectual consciences by reading the legend of Noah's Ark…'

Nevertheless, the vitality of the story in the 20th century is remarkable. Yeats deals with the flood in *The Player Queen;* Marc Connelly devotes three scenes of *The Green Pastures* to the Noah story. For C. Day Lewis in *Noah and the Waters* the deluge serves as a convenient political symbol for breaking with bourgeois liberalism. In *The Skin of Our Teeth* Wilder associates details from the biblical source with a series of different catastrophes, asserting that his archetypal family will begin life again after each one. Odets' *The Flowering Peach* is less optimistic, transforming the narrative into a realistic family drama in which Japheth temporarily rebels against the building of the ark and the brutality of God, and Noah learns that humanity itself can make or destroy the world.

Following Jules Verne's *L'eternel Adam*, some novelists rewrote the biblical story as science fiction, often casting Noah as a scientist and the ark as a spaceship (e.g., Serviss, *The Second Deluge*; Wylie and Balmer, *After Worlds Collide*; and A.C. Clarke, *Rendezvous with Rama* and *The Songs of Distant Earth*). H.G. Wells, in *All Aboard for Ararat*, focuses on a utopian writer who, refusing to act like the biblical Noah, attempts to improve upon God's work by designing blueprints for the New Ark, the reconstruction of society after World War II. Anthony Burgess' *The End of the World News*, a montage of the biographies of Freud and Trotsky, and a parody of Serviss' *The Second Deluge*, makes the point that all designs for the new world will ultimately be mocked. In Vonnegut's satire *Galapagos* a few human beings escape the general ruin of the world to become the ancestors of a smaller-brained and happier race.

Apart from such modernizations of the basic story, some imaginative retellings are noteworthy. David Garnett relates in *Two by Two* how two young girls hide in the ark as stowaways and, after the flood, begin life with two of Noah's renegade grandsons. Timothy Findley's *Not Wanted on the Voyage* deals with the sexual and other tensions in Noah's family, everyday life aboard the ark, the rebellion of Noah's wife, Ham's wife Lucy (Lucifer) and others, and Noah's manipulation of the rainbow miracle after God has failed to answer his prayers.

James Joyce alludes to the deluge and calls attention to associated baptismal symbolism in connection with Father Arnall's sermon and Stephen's wading in the sea in his *Portrait of the Artist as a Young Man*. More idiosyncratic references occur in *Ulysses* and *Finnegans Wake*. In D.H. Lawrence's *The Rainbow* imagery of the flood and new beginning describes the maturation process of Ursula and illuminates Lawrence's attitude towards industrial civilization. Like R.P. Warren in 'Blackberry Winter', Faulkner uses the flood story to characterize the religious sensibility of his African-American characters. Social injustice is the theme of Sillitoe's story 'Noah's Ark', in which two poor boys steal a ride on a Noah's ark roundabout and are chased away by the owner. For Thomas Pynchon the apocalypse in *Gravity's Rainbow* is man-made and the rainbow no longer functions as a covenantal or providential sign.

An actual flood reminds Charles Tomlinson (*The Flood*) of the biblical one, but the nightmare of the end of the world which he and his partner face 'with elate despair' turns out to be a dream after all. Beauty characterizes Rumer Godden's post-flood vision in *In Noah's Ark* (1949): the world lies 'washed and sparkling in the newborn day'. Renewal also climaxes Lorenz Graham's flood story for children: *God Wash the World and Start Again* (1946).

Paul Goetsch
Freiburg Universität, Freiburg, Germany
Marie Michelle Walsh
College of Notre Dame of Maryland

Jacob's Ladder

After his deception of Esau made it necessary for him to flee his home, Jacob stopped for the night on the way to Padan-aram, gathering stones around him for pillows, and lay down to sleep. 'And he dreamed, and behold a ladder set up on the earth, and the top of it reached to heaven: and behold the angels of God ascending and descending on it. And, behold, the Lord stood above it, and said, I am the Lord God of Abraham thy father, and the God of Isaac: the land whereon thou liest, to thee will I give it, and to thy seed' (Genesis 28:12–13). What followed was a confirmation that God's covenant with Abraham had indeed passed to Jacob. When he awoke Jacob declared, 'this is none other but the house of God, and this is the gate of heaven'; although the place had been known as Luz, Jacob renamed it Bethel ('House of God').

In the spiritual literature of the Middle Ages Jacob's ladder becomes an analogue for spiritual growth and progress. Perhaps the most famous application of the image to religious life is that found in the Benedictine Rule, which governed the life of the earliest monastic communities in Britain. Commenting on Luke 14:11 (cf. Psalm 131:1–2), 'whosoever exalteth himself shall be abased, and he that humbleth himself shall be exalted', the author of the Rule argues that the way to heavenly heights is along the steps of humility, beginning with the fear of God and moving through obedience and perseverance in humility to the twelfth degree, in which outward comportment is consonant with inward humility, and to the 'top, the charity which is perfect and casts out all fear'. The way up is the way down. In the preface to his *Ars Praedicandi*, a handbook for preachers, Alain of Lille develops the allusion in Pope Gregory's *Regulae Pastoralis* to say that 'the ladder represents the progress of the catholic man in his ascent from the beginning of faith to the full development of the perfect man'. In this tradition the emphasis (as in the familiar camp-meeting song 'We Are Climbing Jacob's Ladder') is upon ascent alone. Alain associates each of the rungs with a stage in spiritual progress: confession, prayer, thanksgiving, the careful study of scriptures, the pursuit of sound instruction in scriptural exegesis, the expounding of scripture, and, finally, preaching. St Bonaventure's *Itinerarium Mentis in Deum* describes the 'mind's journey to God', using Jacob's ladder to figure the mystical progress of the soul toward union with God, dividing the ascent into 'six stages of the soul's powers by which we mount from the depths to the heights, from the external to the internal, from the temporal to the eternal' (preface). The final moment in such an ascent is utter self-transcendence, in which all fetters of the world fall away and, in Bonaventure's words, 'another Jacob is changed into Israel, so through him all truly spiritual persons have been invited by God to passage of this kind...'. The English title of Walter Hilton's vernacular classic *The Ladder of Perfection* draws upon these same associations.

The chief voices of Reformation commentary follow a basically Augustinian line of interpretation. For Luther, who reviews a substantial body of the medieval commentary from Gregory to Nicholas of Lyra's *Postilla*, the ladder is above all a symbol of the Incarnation (*Lectures on Genesis*, 26–30 [*Weimarer Ausgabe* 43.576–80]); he draws heavily on the traditional juxtaposition of the Jacob narrative with the Nathanael incident (John 1:47–51). For Calvin 'it is Christ alone... who connects heaven and earth: he is the only Mediator who reaches from heaven down to earth: he is the medium through which the fulness of all celestial blessings flows down to us, and through which we, in turn, ascend to God' (*Commentary on Genesis*, 2.28). Cornelius à Lapide cites Theodoret and Ibn Ezra, sources Calvin rejects, to say that the ladder is first of all a symbol for divine providence, with the angels as ministers of providence; allegorically, he says (following Augustine, *Sermo*, 79) the ladder is the cross of Christ and a sign of the incarnation of the Word, while tropologically it is the human spirit, with the descending angels signifying carnal appetite and those ascending representing intellectual and spiritual aspiration. The rungs are virtues in the 'ladder of perfection'. Anagogically, the angels signify the various levels of achievement and orders of the blessed (*Commentarii in Genesim*, 28.286–89).

In one of John Donne's sermons (eds. Potter and Simpson, 3.58), he draws on Lapide to say that God holds his ladder up to heaven 'and all those good works which are put upon the lowest step... that is, that are done in contemplation of him, they ascend to him, and descend to us' (cf. 2.186; 5.264). In *Paradise Lost* (3.510–15) Milton describes what Satan sees at the portal of heaven:

> The Stairs were such as whereon Jacob saw
> Angels ascending and descending, bands
> Of Guardians bright, when he from *Esau* fled
> To *Padan-Aram* in the field of *Luz*,
> Dreaming by night under the open Sky,
> And waking cri'd, *This is the Gate of Heav'n*.

In his essay *The Means to Remove Hirelings* Milton cites Jacob's vow following his dream (Genesis 28:22) as the formal biblical proclamation of tithing as part of service to God, though 'not to any priest'.

Ben Jonson, in celebrating Lady Digby ('LXXXIV Eupheme'), speaks of her

> ... getting up
> By Jacob's ladder, to the top
> Of that eternal port kept ope
> For such as she.

Dryden sees the ladder as a symbol of the progress of culture,

> Where ev'ry age do's on another move,
> And trusts no farther than the next above;
> Where all the rounds like *Jacob's* ladder rise,
> The lowest hid in earth, the topmost in the skyes
> (2.218–21)

– a latitudinarian sentiment, although it appears in his Catholic *The Hind and the Panther*. An intentionally humorous reference is found in Thomas Gray's 'The Characters of Christ-Cross Row', in which the reader is obliged to imagine the corporal bulk of 'his hugeness H... / Henry the Eighth's most monstrous majesty' ascending and descending the ladder in place of angels (21–28). Charles Wesley's hymn,

> What doth the ladder mean
> Sent down from the Most High?
> Fasten'd to earth its foot is seen,
> Its summit to the sky,

while seeming to echo Dryden, is actually indebted to Augustine, Luther, and Calvin:

> Jesus that ladder is,
> Th'incarnate Deity,
> Partaker of celestial bliss,
> And human misery;
> Sent from His high abode,
> To sleeping mortals given,
> He stands, and man unites to God,
> And earth connects to heaven.

Wordsworth's angels are expressions of human aspiration remarkably akin to Dryden's: 'Glorious is the blending / Of right affections climbing or descending / Along a scale of light and life'. The Lake poet's Jacob, however, while sleeping, was also himself 'treading the pendent stairs' ('Humanity', 27–40). Thomas de Quincey argues in his essay 'Literature of Knowledge and Literature of Power' that Milton's is the latter category, promoting the 'exercise and expansion of your own latent capacity of sympathy with the infinite, where every pulse is... a step upwards, a step ascending as upon Jacob's ladder from earth to mysterious altitudes above'. In Robert Browning's 'Fefine at the Fair', the curé's sermon on Jacob's dream of the ladder sets out to

> ... put in proof,
> When we have scaled the sky, we well may let alone
> What raised us from the ground, and – paying to the stone
> Proper respect, of course – take staff and go our way.
> (2108–2111)

In a nice juxtaposition, Hawthorne's Miriam in *The Marble Faun* mounts a serial staircase to the palace which seems to her 'for the loftiness of its aspiration... worthy to be Jacob's ladder, or, at all events, the staircase of the Tower of Babel.'

An analogous scene occurs in Melville's 'The Two Temples', in which the fifty stone steps ascended by the protagonist (reminiscent of the ascent to Solomon's temple) are surmounted by 'another Jacob's ladder' – a figure which in Melville's mind is associated with charity. But while in 'Temple First' the narrator mounts a Jacob's ladder, in 'Temple Second' Richelieu asserts that one sees the ladder only in dreams. The 'lamb-like' man sleeping at the foot of the ship's ladder in *The Confidence-Man* is, presumably in this second sense, likened by Melville to Jacob 'dreaming at Luz'. In Longfellow's *Evangeline* (2.2) the vision is reduced to a rope ladder hanging from a cedar tree, with hovering hummingbirds as angels.

Carlyle has modern, rather than ancient, interpretations of the passage in mind when he writes in *Sartor Resartus*: 'To our young Friend all women were holy, were heavenly... All of air they were, all Soul and Form; so lovely, like mysterious priestesses, in whose hand was the invisible Jacob's ladder, whereby man might mount into very heaven' (2.5). And if ascent of one kind or another had been the aspiration expressed in allusions from the medieval mystics to 18th- and 19th-century liberal and Romantic humanism, Shaw's *Back to Methuselah* returns full circle to a crashing descent. The ex-curate Franklyn Barnabas, proclaiming the 'Gospel of the Brothers Barnabas', includes in his crypto-theology of the fall from Adam and Eve's vegetarian socialism to meat-eating mayhem the following invitation: 'I ask you to contemplate our fathers as they came crashing down all the steps of this Jacob's ladder that reached from paradise to a hell on earth in which they multiplied the chances of death from violence, accident, and disease until they could hardly count on three score and ten years of life, much less the thousand that Adam had been ready to face!'

David L. Jeffrey
University of Ottawa

Serpent

The first instances of the serpent in English literature are clearly derived from Genesis 3, where Satan takes the form of a 'subtle' and beautiful creature to tempt Eve (3:1–6) and is then condemned by God to crawl upon the earth and live in enmity with 'the seed' of the woman (3:14–15). In one of the most influential commentaries on this passage, St Augustine allegorizes the story in such a way that the psychology of temptation is described: Adam stands for *sapientia*, Eve for *scientia*, and the serpent for sensuality, which, when it obtains mastery, subverts wisdom, confounds knowledge, and inverts their ordinate relationship (*De Trinitate* 12.12.17; see also *De Genesi ad litteram*). References to the serpent in Exodus 4:3 (the rod of Moses, transformed by God in order that the Hebrews would 'believe that the Lord God of their fathers, the God of Abraham, the God of Isaac, and the God of Jacob, hath appeared unto thee') and to the brazen serpent set up by Moses in the wilderness as a means of healing for those bitten by serpents (Numbers 21:8–9; 2 Kings 18:4; cf. John 3:14) are also important. The most important New Testament citation is Christ's sending out of his apostles with the injunction that they be 'wise as serpents, harmless as doves' (Matthew 10:16). In the book of

Revelation (12:9; 20:2) Satan is referred to as both 'dragon' and 'serpent', designations which persist in subsequent literature (the celebrated and sinister dragon of the Old English *Beowulf* is referred to throughout the poem as both *draca*, 'dragon', and *wyrm*, 'serpent').

The Genesis episode has a central place in Milton's *Paradise Lost* and *Paradise Regained*, where several departures from the biblical account invoke ancient associations of gnostic wisdom with the serpent. The most important of these is in book 9 of *Paradise Lost*, where Satan's approach to Eve, in the body of the serpent, is filled with sinister allure:

> ... Oft he bow'd
> His turret Crest, and sleek enamell'd Neck,
> Fawning, and lick'd the ground whereon she trod.
> His gentle dumb expression turn'd at length
> The Eye of *Eve* to mark his play; he glad
> Of her attention gain'd, with Serpent Tongue
> Organic, or impulse of vocal Air,
> His fraudulent temptation thus began.
> (*Patrologia Latina*, 9.524–31)

Eve is surprised to hear the serpent speak: 'Thee, Serpent, subtlest beast of all the field / I knew, but not with human voice endu'd' (9.560–61). Elsewhere in *Paradise Lost*, Sin, one of the two guardians (with Death) of the gates of Hell, is described as

> Woman to the waist, and fair,
> But ended foul in many a scaly fold
> Voluminous and vast, a Serpent arm'd
> With mortal sting. (2.650–53)

This description nicely conforms to Renaissance pictorial representations of the serpent about to tempt Eve in the garden (e.g., Cranach's 'Temptation' or Bosch's 'Haywain' triptych).

Blake develops a central place for the serpent in his own alternative mythology. Northrop Frye observes that 'Orc, or human imagination trying to burst out of the body, is often described as a serpent bound on the tree of mystery, dependent upon it, yet struggling to get free' (*Fearful Symmetry*, 136). For Blake the serpent shedding its skin symbolizes immortality, and he is happy to conflate the brazen serpent with that in Eden, or with the dragon of the Apocalypse, as occasion permits. These conflations appear in simple lyrics such as his 'Infant Sorrow', but enlarge and gain complexity in larger works such as *The Four Zoas*.

In Byron's *Cain* the serpent's insinuations are given new credibility:

> The snake spoke truth; it was the tree of knowledge;
> It was the tree of life: knowledge is good,
> And life is good; and how can both be evil?
> (*Cain*, 1.36–38)

Tennyson and Browning employ the Genesis commonplace straightforwardly. The curse of the serpent is a popular motif in the writings of Swinburne, who manipulates it to serve secular, typically political ends ('The Armada', 'A Song of Italy', 'A Counsel'). Conrad makes complex symbolic use of the same motif in *Victory* and *The Secret Agent*.

The serpent or snake, since the time of Augustine an image of sensuality, is in the modern period increasingly associated with sexuality and sexual licence. D.H. Lawrence in *The Plumed Serpent* describes the fascination of Kate Leslie, a restless and unfulfilled Irish widow, with a revived Mexican serpent-cult, its dark and elemental rituals an explicit repudiation of Christianity. Joyce's Stephen calls the sexual organ to which he has become subservient 'the serpent, the most subtle beast of the field' (*A Portrait of the Artist as a Young Man*, chapter 3).

A more complex evocation of the serpent of Genesis, and one of the central scenes in the Faulkner myth, is found in 'The Bear' from *Go Down, Moses*, in which the snake is described as 'the ancient and accursed about the earth, fatal and solitary':

> he could smell it now: the thin smell of rotting cucumbers and something else which had no name, evocative of all knowledge and an old weariness and of pariah-hood and of death. At last it moved. Not the head. The elevation of the head did not change as it began to glide away from him,

moving erect yet off the perpendicular as if the head and that
elevated third were complete and all: an entity walking on
two feet and free of all laws of mass and balance and should
have been because even now he could not quite believe that
all that shift and flow of shadow behind that walking head
could have been one snake.

Mark Twain twists and even reverses the Genesis passage in his later
writings, most particularly in his *Diary of Adam* and *Diary of Eve*, while
in *Letters from the Earth* he gives Satan's point of view on the events of
the Fall. Langston Hughes offers a tongue-in-cheek rejoinder to the
whole tradition of the Fall as occasioned by the serpent in his
'Temptation', where Simple points out to the supposedly more
'learned' narrator:

> I am not talking about no symbol... I am talking about the
> day when Eve took the apple and Adam et. From then on
> the human race has been in trouble. There ain't a coloured
> woman living what would take no apple from a snake – and
> she better not give no snake-apples to her husband.

Robert Farrell
Cornell University
Catherine Karkov
Miami University of Ohio

Sodom and Gomorrah

Sodom and Gomorrah were among the five 'cities of the plain'
(Genesis 14:2) in the Jordan River valley which God destroyed for
their iniquity when not even ten righteous men could be found there
(Genesis 18:16–19:29). Although to this day Sodom and Gomorrah
together represent human depravity or divine judgment because they
are thus linked in biblical prophetic warnings (Isaiah 1:9; 13:19;
Jeremiah 23:14; 49:18; Amos 4:11; Zephaniah 2:9; Matthew 10:15;
Romans 9:29; Jude 7), the reputation is chiefly Sodom's: no legend
of Gomorrah survives. Among the sins of Sodom are its lack of justice
(Isaiah 1:9–10; 3:9); backsliding into idolatry (Deuteronomy

32:15–43; Isaiah 1:10; expressed through the metaphor of adultery in Jeremiah 23:14); 'pride, fulness of bread, and abundance of idleness', disregard for the poor, and whoring after false gods (Ezekiel 16:49–50). In rabbinic literature, Sodom is known for greed and Procrustean inhospitality to strangers (Pirqe de Rabbi Eliezer, 25).

The homosexuality of the Sodomites (whence 'sodomy') is referred to in Genesis 19:5, where the men of Sodom are said to congregate around Lot's house and demand that he send out two male houseguests, 'that we may know them' (cf. Judges 19:22–24). Lot, horrified by their wicked intentions (19:7), offers his virgin daughters instead but is himself threatened with violence. The visitors, revealing themselves to Lot as angels, strike the men of Sodom with blindness and pronounce God's judgment upon the city.

The sexual sin of Sodom is spoken of in Jubilees 16:5–6 and Testament of Naphtali 3:4–5, as well as in 2 Peter 2:4, 6–8 and Jude 6–7. Philo condemns the sexual perversity of Sodom (e.g., *Quaestiones et solutiones in Genesim*, 4.37–38).

In English literature there are many treatments of the Sodom and Gomorrah story, all of which, until the 20th century, stay close to traditional lines. In addition, there are numerous allusions, though few in which 'Sodom and Gomorrah' is anything more than a byword. The Old English *Genesis* (1920–2162, 2399–2599) and the Middle English *Genesis and Exodus* (837–942, 1050–1122) both include Abraham's wars in defence of Sodom (Genesis 14) and the destruction; *Genesis and Exodus* also describes the Dead Sea region (1123–32). *Cursor Mundi* includes, in addition, a moralization (2491–2547, 2765–2912). A similar but much briefer account is in *A Middle English Metrical Paraphrase of the Old Testament* (571–616; ed. H. Kalén, Göteborgs Högskolas Årsskrift, 28.5, 1922). Langland's use of Sodom and Gomorrah as an example of luxury in Pacience's speech on charity and patient poverty (*Piers Plowman*, B.14.73–81; C.16.231–33) follows Ezekiel 16:49; Chaucer's *The Parson's Tale*, 10.839, follows Genesis 19:5 and Jude 7. In *Cleanness* the literal and figurative sterility of Sodom's homosexuality and faithlessness is a chief instance of the uncleanness against which the poet preaches and is symbolized by the apples of Sodom (671–1048).

The broadside ballad 'Of the Horrible and Woefull Destruction of Sodom and Gomorrah' (1570) describes the suffering of the Sodomites in the rain of fire and brimstone, then urges Englishmen to amend their lives lest they should suffer likewise. In George Lesley's verse drama 'Fire and Brimstone' (*Divine Dialogues*, 1678), the Sodomites decide to beg the angels for mercy, but too late; they lament their sins as their city burns, and the play closes with a choral exhortation to avoid lust and gluttony. The hero of Marlowe's *Tamburlaine* climaxes his career as scourge of God by capturing Babylon and ordering the drowning of all its inhabitants in Lake Asphaltites (2 *Tamburlaine*, 5.1). In the peroration of 'Reason of Church Government', Milton likens 'prelaty' to Sodom and Gomorrah (*Complete Poems and Major Prose*, 1957, 689). Milton assigns Belial, angel of lust and violence, to Sodom (*Paradise Lost*, 1.503–505) and has the devils, metamorphosed into snakes, eat of the apples of Sodom as punishment for tempting Adam and Eve (10.560–77). Following Milton, Blake makes Belial chief of Sodom and Gomorrah, one of the twelve synagogues of Satan, in *Milton*, 37.30–32. In *Jerusalem*, 67.40, Sodom and Gomorrah are among the many loci in the vessels of the circulatory system joined to the heart of the Polypus of Generation, the worldly society which is 'the antithesis of the Brotherhood of Man' (S.F. Damon, *Blake Dictionary*, 33). For Byron's Childe Harold the thought that

> ... life will suit
> Itself to Sorrow's most detested fruit,
> Like to the apples on the Dead Sea's shore,
> All ashes to the taste

arises from contemplating the return of spring at the Waterloo battlefield and the loss there of his friend Howard (*Childe Harold's Pilgrimage*, 3.34.4–7).

Melville alludes several times to Sodom and Gomorrah as a symbol of sexual depravity or of catastrophe (*White Jacket*, chapter 89; *Israel Potter*, chapter 19; *Redburn*, chapter 31); but in *Moby Dick* the allusions portend the destruction of the Pequod and Ishmael's Lot-like escape (chapters 2, 9, 117). Browning's vision of Christ 'Like the smoke / Pillared o'er Sodom, when day broke', in *Easter-Day* (640–41) foreshadows his being sentenced to the world for eternity because all his life he chose the world. For Lord Lufton in Trollope's *Framley Parsonage*, marriage to the girl Lucy will be like tasting the Dead Sea fruit because 'the sweetest morsel of love's feast has been eaten... when the ceremony at the altar has been performed, and legal possession has been given' (chapter 48). In Twain's *Mysterious Stranger* (chapter 8), Satan's 'history of the progress of the human race' includes Sodom and Gomorrah in its relentless series of murders and wars. The focus here is not the destruction of Sodom and Gomorrah but the 'attempt to find two or three respectable persons there'. In Lawrence's story 'Things', Valerie and Erasmus Melville regard America as 'the Sodom and Gomorrah of industrial materialism', but the image reflects back on them, since their European life is a Sodom and Gomorrah of cultural materialism.

Departing from tradition, Maria Ley-Piscator's novel *Lot's Wife* (1956) relates a fictional life of Lot and his wife, Ti-sar-ilani, which explains why she looks back at Sodom as it burns: in order to define herself existentially and participate in divine justice. Completely drained of biblical significance, Isaac Bashevis Singer's short story 'The Interview' (*New Yorker*, 16 May 1983, 41–48) uses Sodom and Gomorrah as an image for the personal sexual unhappiness of one woman and for the general misery of Jewish history.

M.W. Twomey
Ithaca College

Tree of Knowledge

The tree of the knowledge of good and evil, literally 'the tree of [the] knowing good and evil' (Genesis 2:9, 17) was planted, with the tree of life, in the midst of the Garden of Eden, and was uniquely prohibited: 'But of the tree of the knowledge of good and evil, thou shalt not eat of it; for in the day that thou eatest thereof thou shalt surely die' (Genesis 2:17).

From ancient times, interpretation of this powerful but ambiguous symbol has divided on fundamental questions: What does the tree represent? Does eating of it merely produce sinful alienation, or does it, as the Gnostics were later to imagine, involve some positive knowledge, and, if so, of what kind? The exact Hebrew phrase used in the Genesis account does not appear elsewhere in the Old Testament. In other passages, however, 'knowing' good and evil seems to imply a level of maturity (Deuteronomy 1:39), and moral (or more general) discernment and judgment (2 Samuel 14:17; 19:35; 1 Kings 3:9; Hebrews 5:14), but there is no necessary connection between these passages and the Genesis tree.

St Augustine gave currency to the most influential interpretation, in which the tree represents allegorically 'the free choice of our own will' (*De civitate Dei* 13.21) and in which its name signifies 'what good [Adam and Eve] would experience if they kept the prohibition or what evil if they transgressed it' (*De peccatorum meritis et remissione*, 2.35; *De civitate Dei*, 14.17). This interpretation remained normative throughout the Reformation. Calvin similarly sees the tree as a 'proof and exercise' of man's faith (*Institutes*, 2.1.4); Luther speculates that it may well have been a grove, as a 'temple of divine worship', in effect 'Adam's church, altar, and pulpit', and the prohibition concerning it a pre-Fall ritual law enabling humanity to demonstrate its obedience (*Lectures on Genesis*, on Genesis 2:9, 17).

This tradition culminates memorably in Milton's *Paradise Lost*. For Milton, as for Augustine, the tree is potent not in itself but as the 'sole pledge' of man's obedience (3.95; 8.325), and the knowledge gained from eating of it merely, as Adam bitterly complains, of 'Good lost, and Evil got' (9.1072). Moreover, in describing the temptation and fall of Eve (9.568–838), Milton gathers and enhances traditional interpretive details concerning the tree: it is beautiful, attracting all the senses; it stimulates (with the prompting of Satan) Eve's impatient ambition to be like God; its fair appearance (together with Satan's plausible analogies) is deceptive – Eve's first act after eating is to worship the power which 'dwelt within' the tree, not to worship God.

Prior to Milton the tree was used by Chaucer, whose Pardoner sees in Adam's sin only gluttony (*Pardoner's Tale*, 6.505–512) and whose Parson describes Eve's temptation in terms of 'the beautee of the fruyt' (*Parson's Tale*, 10.325–29). An analysis of the tree considered from the literal, allegorical, tropological, and anagogical perspectives of medieval fourfold exegesis occurs in Langland's *Piers Plowman* (B.16.1–89). But far more common is the legend identifying the tree with the holy rood. This connection originates in the patristic interpretation of Adam as a type of Christ and the tree as a type of the cross (St John Chrysostom, *Homily on Romans*, 10.13–14). According to the *Cursor Mundi*, Seth received from an angel three seeds from the tree, seeds of cedar, cypress, and palm (corresponding to Father, Son, and Holy Ghost). These were planted, and Adam was buried beneath the trees which grew from them; David later found them grown together into a single tree of miraculous power. This tree resisted cutting for Solomon's temple and was thrown into a pool which became a place of healing (cf. Exodus 15:25). Later, having been preserved in the Temple until Christ's coming, it was made into the cross. The identification of the tree with the cross is widespread in medieval lyrics, and still survives in Luther (*Lectures on Genesis*, 4:16) and Donne ('Hymn to God, My God, in My Sickness').

By the time Milton was producing the richest traditional consideration of the tree, others had begun to disregard or demythologize it. Sir Thomas Browne (*Pseudodoxia Epidemica*, 1) mentions as an irresolvable talmudic speculation 'whether the tree in the midst of the garden, were not that part in the centre of the body, in which was afterward the appointment of circumcision in males'. Dryden jokes that 'had our grandsire [Adam] walk'd without his wife / He first had sought the better plant of life!' ('To My Honor'd Kinsman, John Driden', 98–99); and Marvell, with casual irony, wishes that a learned decedent had 'on the Tree of Life once made a feast / As that of Knowledge' ('Upon the Death of Lord Hastings', 19–20). Similarly satirical is Cowper's analogy between the tree and the popular press: 'Like Eden's dread probationary tree / Knowledge of good and evil is from thee' ('Progress of Error', 468–69).

The tree's symbolic power is rediscovered and reconfigured by the Romantics and their heirs, who tend to view it less as reflecting a choice humanity has made or makes than a condition to which he is (tragically) subject. It is frequently associated by William Blake with mankind's fall from innocent appetite into a satanic state of obsession with the rational, legal, and moral. Thus in *Jerusalem* one finds (pl. 28, 1.15) the 'deadly Tree' of Albion, 'Moral Virtue and the Law', and in the marginalia on Bacon's 'Of Truth', 'Self Evident Truth is one Thing and Truth the result of Reasoning is another Thing. Rational Truth is not the Truth of Christ, but of Pilate. It is the Tree of the Knowledge of Good and Evil'. In *The Four Zoas* (Nights 7–9) it becomes a 'Tree of Mystery' with 'shining globes' of various poisons, among them passionate love and sorrow, to which the lamb is later nailed (the medieval legend revived) and which is burned at the Last Judgment. Shelley reduces the tree to a 'tree of evil' planted for man's misery by a malicious creator ('Queen Mab', 8.108–114).

Perhaps the most influential modern use has been that of Byron, who, in his poetic dramas *Cain* and *Manfred*, draws on it for a tragic image of humanity's mixed condition. He reflects on Milton's observation in *Areopagitica*, that 'It was from out the rind of one apple tasted, that the knowledge of good and evil, as two twins cleaving together, leaped forth into the world. And perhaps this is that doom which Adam fell into of knowing good and evil, that is to say, of knowing good by evil'; Byron thus sees good and evil, life and grief, knowledge and sorrow as indissolubly bound together. In *Manfred*:

> ... grief should be the instructor of the wise
> Sorrow is knowledge: they who know the most
> Must mourn the deepest o'er the fatal truth
> The Tree of Knowledge is not that of Life. (1.1.9–12)

Later writers have treated this theme in several moods, from the stoic irony of Henry James' story 'The Tree of Knowledge', in which an older man, in trying to preserve the innocence of a young friend, loses the sustaining illusion of his own life, to the comic, vitalist vehemence of Shaw, who declares that, in Adam's place, he would

> have swallowed every apple on the tree the moment the owner's back was turned... it is godlike to be wise... it is stupid, and indeed blasphemous and despairing, to hope that the thirst for knowledge will either diminish or consent to be subordinated to any other end whatsoever. (*Doctor's Dilemma*, preface)

In the demotic prometheanism of MacLeish's *Nobodaddy* or Louis Untermeyer's 'Eve Speaks', eating of the tree is defended as necessary in order that 'Adam should know his godhood; he should feel / The weariness of work, and pride of it / The agony of creation, and its reward.'

The tree continues to suggest the mystery attending many kinds of innocence and experience, various Edens to be gained, maintained, or lost. Carlyle remarks that

> In every well-conditioned stripling, as I conjecture, there already blooms a certain prospective Paradise, cheered by some fairest Eve; nor, in the stately vistas, and flowery foliage of that Garden, is a Tree of Knowledge, beautiful and awful in the midst thereof, wanting. (*Sartor Resartus*, 2.5)

In *Where There Is Nothing*, Yeats comments (in a gnostic inversion of Paul) on the intimate connection between law and sin: 'they thought it would be better to be safe than to be blessed, they made the Laws. The Laws were the first sin. They were the first mouthful of the apple, the moment man had made them he began to die' (299–303). In his poem 'The Two Trees', biblical and Celtic associations are combined to produce two mysterious trees, the 'holy' one of life and love and a 'fatal' one, barren and demonic, through whose 'broken branches, go / The ravens of unresting thought'. T.S. Eliot's reflection on the 'wrath-bearing Tree' in 'Gerontion' is more particularly mindful of biblical tradition in the question it poses: 'After such knowledge, what forgiveness?'

Robert Wiltenburg
Washington University

Major Characters

Abel

Abel, whose name may derive from the Hebrew word *hebel*, meaning 'breath', was the brother of Cain and second son of Adam and Eve; his story is told in Genesis 4:1–10.

In the New Testament, Abel appears in three contexts: (a) in Matthew 23:35 and Luke 11:51 he is named as the first martyr to have shed blood; (b) in Hebrews 11:4 (cf. 1 John 3:12) his righteousness, manifest when God accepts his offering, leads to his enrolment as the earliest of those who acted 'by faith'; and (c) in Hebrews 12:24 he appears as a prefigurative type of Christ, although the latter's shedding of blood 'speaketh better things than that of Abel'.

In contrast to his stature among theologians, Abel is decidedly a minor figure in English literature. In *Hamlet*, the king likens himself to Cain in a soliloquy which confesses: 'My offense is rank, it smells to heaven; / It hath the primal eldest curse upon't, / A brother's murder' (3.3.36–38). In *Richard II*, Henry Bolingbroke accuses Thomas Mowbray of having murdered the Duke of Gloucester, whose blood, 'like sacrificing Abel's, cries... to me for justice' (1.1.104–106). By the end of this play, however, Henry is himself indirectly guilty of the murder of Richard and promises a pilgrimage to the Holy Land to wash the blood from *his* hand; at the same time he consigns Exton, the slayer, to 'go wander' with Cain. The patristic tradition which has Damascus as the place of Abel's murder is reflected in *Henry VI (1)* when the Bishop of Winchester, posing as an innocent Abel, says to his enemy the Duke of Gloucester: 'Nay, stand thou back, I will not budge a foot; / This be Damascus, be thou cursed Cain, / To slay thy brother Abel, if thou wilt' (1.3.38–40).

Henry Vaughan's 'Abel's Blood' in part 2 of *Silex Scintillans*, an ardent Royalist's meditation on lives lost in the civil wars, opens with Abel's blood crying to heaven and modulates to Christ's 'milde blood' of atonement which, as John Diodati observes in a note on Hebrews 12:24, 'presents it selfe before God, not to desire vengeance of the murtherous Jews, as *Abels* did against Cain, *Genesis* 4.10, but to obtain favour and pardon for them' (*Pious Annotations upon the Holy Bible*, 1681). The same theme appears in two quatrains (203 and 204) in Herrick's *His Noble Numbers*.

Milton's treatment of the Cain and Abel story in *Paradise Lost* (11.429–47) is largely conventional, although the imagery subtly links Abel (who places his sacrifice 'on the cleft Wood') with Christ, and Cain 'the sweaty Reaper' with the infernal triad of Satan, Sin, and Death. The most original and perplexing use of Abel in Renaissance literature is in Donne's 'The Progresse of the Soule' (1601), a fragmentary mock-epic poem tracing the history of a 'deathlesse' soul through a series of incarnations from the forbidden apple plucked by Eve, through plants, birds, and fish, to a wolf (401–428) which seduces Abel's bitch in order to prey on the sheep until he is killed in one of Abel's traps, then passes to the offspring (428–50) of the wolf and Abel's bitch, a schizoid beast which both protects and eats the herd, and then finally passes into the body of Themech, 'sister and wife to *Caine*' (510). Ben Jonson (*Works*, 1.136) says Donne's 'generall purpose was to have brought in all the bodies of the Hereticks from the soule of Caine & at last left it in the body of Calvin'.

References in the 18th century are few and uninteresting – Pope, *Essay on Man*, 4.118; Cowper, 'Hope', 644, Burns 'On the Late Captain Grose's Peregrinations Thro' Scotland', 44–48.

English translations of Salomon Gessner's prose epic *Der Tod Abels* (1758), coupled with the general Romantic interest in the psychology of guilt and remorse, led to a revival of interest in the Cain and Abel story in the early 19th century. The common feature of these versions is the secularization of the theme, the use of biblical event and language for psychological, aesthetic, even political, ends. In Coleridge's Gothic fragment 'The Wanderings of Cain', the ghost of Abel confronts Cain as an externalization of guilt-ridden conscience; in Byron's *Cain: A Mystery*, the pious Abel dies with Christ's words from the cross (Luke 23:34, 46) on his lips: 'Oh, God! receive thy servant, and / Forgive his slayer, for he knew not what / He did' (3.318–20); in Shelley's political drama *Hellas*, the Turkish sultan Mahmud opines that the Spirit of fallen Greeks cries against him for vengeance 'like the blood of Abel from the dust' (355). In Blake's theophanic 'Ghost of Abel', the visionary poet cries out, through Abel, in defence of the creative imagination.

Post-Romantic references to Abel tend to be conventional. In George Eliot's *Middlemarch*, the only thing Mr Bulstrode can say about Abel, his shepherd-bailiff at Stone Court, is that he 'has done well with the lambs this year' (chapter 69). More recently, John Updike has penned his own version of the Abel story in 'The Invention of the Horse Collar' (*Museums and Women*), where Abel (Ablatus) represents a personalized society destined to give in to the way of Cain (Canus) in technological revolution.

John Spencer Hill
University of Ottawa

Abraham

The biography of Abraham, first of the Hebrew patriarchs, is recorded in Genesis 11:26 – 25:18.

In the New Testament Abraham is recognized as the father of Israel and of the Levitical priesthood (Hebrews 7), as the 'legal' forebear of Jesus (i.e., ancestor of Joseph according to Matthew 1), and spiritual progenitor of all Christians (Romans 4; Galatians 3:16, 29; cf. also the *Visio Pauli*). For St Paul, Abraham is the chief Old Testament type of Christian faith because he 'believed God, and it was counted unto him for righteousness' (Romans 4:3) – before the law of Moses, before the requirement of circumcision, before the establishment of any religious ritual.

In English literary tradition, the Abraham narrative has a diverse and colourful history. More than one-third of the Caedmonian *Genesis* is devoted to the story of Abraham and his clan, with emphasis throughout on the various forms of God's covenant (*treowe*). The poem ends with an account of the sacrifice of Isaac. In early English literature the promises made to Abraham are exploited in complex ways in relation to the fulfilment of the promises in Christ. In the Old English *Exodus*, stories of both Noah and Abraham appear in connection with the narrative of the crossing of the Red Sea because of the typological relationship of all three stories to the atonement. For Milton, Abraham's seed is the 'great deliverer, who shall bruise / The

Serpent's head' (*Paradise Lost*, 12.149–50; cf. Genesis 3:15). Marlowe's Barabas perverts the notion of God's promises to Abraham when he says that material goods are 'the blessings promised to the Jews / And herein was old Abram's happiness' (*The Jew of Malta*, 1.1.106).

Langland's *Piers Plowman* accords Abraham a significant role as Faith in search of the Trinity and of Christ's Church (B.16ff.), and the dreamer there is given a somewhat confusing account of Abraham's life from the patriarch himself. In *Andreas*, as in its model, the apocryphal Acts of Andrew, Abraham is 'resurrected' from the dead so that he can explain the nature of the Trinity to Jews. *Cleanness* devotes a lengthy passage to paraphrasing Abraham's meeting with the angelic visitors, primarily in order to contrast Abraham's goodness with the wickedness of the citizens of Sodom, but presenting also a noteworthy treatment of the triune God. A famous visual representation of the Old Testament trinity is the early 15th-century icon by the Russian Andrei Rubler.

The offering of Isaac is a crucial subject in medieval religious drama. The incident is also dramatized in the French *mystères*. French Calvinist theologian Theodore Beza composed an influential play on the subject, *Abraham Sacrifiant* (1550), which was subsequently translated into English by Arthur Golding (1577) to teach 'the mightie power of earnest faith / And what reward the true obedience payth'. Henry Fielding treats the incident comically in *Joseph Andrews*, where Parson Abraham Adams (who, like his biblical namesake, spends much of his time wandering) is unable to accept the (erroneous) news of his son's death, even while he is lecturing on the subject of Abraham's willingness to sacrifice Isaac. Blake's *Book of Urizen* reflects the incident ironically in Los' willing sacrifice of Orc. In *Tess of the D'Urbervilles* Hardy compares the love of Mr Clare for his son Angel to the love of Abraham for Isaac.

In his *Castle of Indolence* James Thomson presents an eccentric picture of Abraham's wanderings as a time of idyllic happiness. The nomadic life of Abraham and his large progeny form the basis of Faulkner's comparison to him of the character Flem Snopes (in *Sartoris*), although the likeness is ironic in view of Flem's impotence. *Father Abraham* was the title of an early version of some of the material of Faulkner's *The Hamlet*. One of the two occasions on which Abraham suppressed the information that Sarah was his wife (Genesis 12; 20) is used by Walter Scott to characterize the Countess of Leicester in *Kenilworth* (chapter 22). Margaret Laurence's *The Stone Angel* chronicles the life of Hagar Shipley and her husband Bram (from Abram) and explores many of the themes of the Genesis narrative in contemporary terms.

Phillip Rogers
Queen's University, Kingston, Ontario

Adam

Curiously, *Adam* as a proper noun does not assuredly occur in the Hebrew text of Genesis until well after the Garden of Eden story. In 4:25 the word occurs as a proper name for the first time: 'Adam lay with his wife again'. Throughout the previous passage, the character is referred to simply as 'the man', which of course is the definition of *Adam*.

The etymology of the word is not certain. Josephus (*Antiquities* 1.1.2) thought that it was formed from the Hebrew root *adom*, 'to be red'. Comparative Semitic philology has suggested that the word is related to an Ethiopic word meaning 'the fair one', or Arabic 'creatures', or South Arabic 'servant, slave', or Akkadian 'maker, producer'. Now, even a Sumerian origin for the word, by way of the Hebrew word *dam*, 'blood', is claimed (*Beth Miqra*, 30, 1984–85, 510–13). The numerous possibilities indicate the difficulty of the matter. The Hebrew text (Genesis 2:7) relates the name to *adamah*, 'ground, soil', but this is but one of the many *jeu de mots* characteristic of this particular writer, who puns outrageously and delightfully, as in 2:24, *arummim* ('naked'), and in the very next sentence, 3:1, *arum* ('wise', referring to the snake).

The Adam story of Genesis 2 and 3 is most closely related to ancient Near Eastern stories like Adapa, sage of Eridu, who, although acquiring great wisdom, nevertheless lost an opportunity for immortality. Gilgamesh, too, great and wise though he was, lost immortality to a serpent. In the biblical account, the man and his wife 'became like gods' (3:21) by eating of the tree of knowledge of good and evil and consequently were driven away from the tree of life lest they should also achieve immortality (3:21–22).

Many of the familiar Adamic themes of later literature first make their appearance in the Jewish writings which separate the Hebrew Bible from the New Testament. In the Life of Adam and Eve, a pseudepigraphal work, parts of which are also known as The Apocalypse of Moses and different recensions of which reached the west through Christian mediation by way of the Gospel of Nicodemus and the Latin *Vita Adae et Evae*, Satan says that it was because of Adam that he was banished from heaven and that his hatred and envy of Adam are justified on that account. Also in this ancient book appears for the first time the tradition of Seth's search for the oil of life which will heal his dying father. Seth does not find the oil, and Adam dies, but not before revealing the future to Seth (see Josephus, *Antiquities*, 1.2.3; the Coptic Apocalypse of Adam, 64:2–6; and the Armenian 'Death of Adam', *Harvard Theological Review*, 59, 1966, 283–91). In some accounts, Satan is jealous because Michael commands all angels to worship Adam; in others, he is jealous because the earth is to be subject to Adam (Slavonic Enoch, 31; Wisdom of Solomon, 2:23–24).

The most significant contribution of New Testament writers in the development of the Adam of Western literature is the Adam/Messiah typology, and for this St Paul is chiefly responsible. Paul might well have learned in his Jewish education that Adam was the ideal man and that the Messiah would someday restore all that humanity lost in the Fall, but he is the first writer to see an explicit connection in the two concepts or, as he puts it, to see Adam as 'a type of the one to come' (Romans 5:14). Through the first Adam came sin and death; through the second came grace (Romans 5:12–21); through the one came the death of the body; through the other came resurrection (1 Corinthians 15:20–23); in the 'first Adam' man became an animate being (this based on Paul's midrashic rendering of the Septuagint of Genesis 2:7); in the 'last Adam' man will become a 'spiritual body' in the resurrection (1 Corinthians 15:44–49). Elsewhere in the New Testament Luke traces the genealogy of Jesus to Adam (chapter 3), whereas Matthew begins with Abraham. Mark's account of the temptation of Jesus, with its wild beasts and angels, is very suggestive of the Adam of the Midrash.

Early English literature typically tends to objectify or externalize earlier abstract or metaphorical ideas. Thus Genesis B, the oldest English text treating the subject of Adam's sin, repeatedly emphasizes his literal 'uprightness', his physical standing in his prelapsarian state, and his literal 'falling' to the ground upon eating of the forbidden fruit. This text also explicitly refers to the 'tree of knowledge' as the 'tree of death'.

This same tendency toward literalness underscores the popular medieval legends concerning the Holy Rood, in which the wood of the cross was believed to have been taken from the tree of knowledge. The early 14th-century poem *Cursor Mundi* includes the tradition that Seth, after journeying to the Garden of Eden for the oil of life for Adam, who was dying in Hebron, brought back instead three kernels of the tree of knowledge, which he planted in the mouth of his father upon his death. These trees in turn provide the wood for the cross.

The fully christianized version of the Jewish Life of Adam and Eve comes to us through Middle English writers. This tradition of the cross, of course, is an extension of Paul's Adam / Christ typology, which produced a whole complex of such symmetries: just as Eve listened to the serpent and brought death, so Mary attended the angel and brought forth life; just as Adam disobeyed in the Garden of Eden, so Christ obeyed in the Garden of Gethsemane, etc. Most of these parallels go back to the Fathers (see, e.g., Irenaeus, *Proof of the Apostolic Preaching*, chapter 34).

In the rich poetic tradition of the Middle English period Adam appears chiefly as the means by which sorrow afflicted the human race: 'Adam alas and waylaway! / A luther dede dedest thou that day!' A 'Doomsday' poem of the 13th century asserts, 'From that adam was i-wrout that / comet domesday'. Even children's songs and lullabies such as 'Lollai little child, why weepest thou so sore?' locate the source of all grief in Adam's sin: 'This woe Adam thee wrought / When he of the apple ate.'

Yet this 'woe' is to be gloriously redressed, according to countless lyrics:

Also Adam wyt lust and likynge
Broghte al his ken into wo and wepynge,
So schal a child of the kende springe,
That schal brynge hym and alle hyse
Into joye and blisse habbynge.

The Fall as a *'felix culpa'* – the paradoxical phrase comes from the Easter liturgy – is most clearly seen in the well-known 15th-century 'Adam lay i-bowndyn', which leaves no doubt concerning the beneficent effect of the Fall: 'Blyssid be the tyme that appil take was, / Therefore we mown syngyn *"Deo gracias!"'* But the theological formulation most formative of this relation, and still echoing in the 15th century, is that of St Anselm of Canterbury, whose 12th-century *Cur Deus Homo, si Adam non pecasset* is a groundbreaking theology of the Incarnation. Anselm's influence upon the sermon literature and lyrics of the Franciscans in particular is evident in English allusions to the subject after the 13th century.

Middle English lyrics and drama rehearse the familiar harrowing of hell tradition, as do authors such as Chaucer, who also embraces, or at least echoes, the Augustinian doctrine of original sin:

Loo Adam, in the feeld of Damyssene
With Goddes owene fynger wroght was he,
And nat bigeten of mannes sperme unclene.
(*The Monk's Tale*, 7.207–209)

The matter is quite explicit in *The Parson's Tale*:

'Of thilke Adam tooke we thilke synne original; for of hym flesshly descended be we alle, and engendered of vile and corrupt mateere.'

By the end of the Middle Ages, the simple account of Adam's life given in Genesis had been overlaid with an elaborate mythology, detailing practically everything from the fall of the angels to the precise identification of the fruit of the tree of knowledge. All this became the subject of the mystery plays, which were chiefly associated with the Feast of Corpus Christi. The Fall of Adam was dramatically presented in the York, Chester, and N-Town (Coventry) cycles and probably in the incomplete Wakefield (Towneley) cycle, as well as in the sole survivor of some twelve plays performed in Norwich in the 15th and 16th centuries, now known as the Norwich Grocers' Play. Although most of the material in these plays is familiar, occasionally a new twist on the subject appears, such as the dulling of Adam's and Eve's senses after eating of the fruit: 'A lord for synne oure flourys do ffade / I here thi voys but I see the nought' (N-Town, 275–76). The second play of the Chester cycle contains the relatively novel idea of Adam's dream, which grew out of the simple statement that God put Adam to sleep when he took the rib to make woman. In this dream, which Adam later relates to Cain and Abel, the great flood, the incarnation, and the last judgment are prophesied. The early Syriac Testament of Adam contains a similar scheme: creation, the flood, incarnation, and judgment – communicated by Adam to Seth, not to Cain and Abel. At the heart of these plays is a concern to dramatize the standard Adam / Christ typology. Thus, in the 'Annunciation' play of the Wakefield cycle, for example, God proclaims,

> I wyll that my son manhede take,
> ffor reson wyll that ther be thre,
> A man, a madyn, and a tre;
> Man for man, tre for tre,
> Madyn for madyn, thus shal it be. (30–34)

Edmund Spenser characteristically fuses Adam and the Adam tradition to classical culture in his *Faerie Queene*. Una's parents rule over 'Eden' (1.12.26.1), 'which Phison and Euphrates floweth by, / And Gehons golden waues doe wash continually' (1.7.43.8–9; cf. Genesis 2:11–14). After long exclusion from their native land, they are restored to it by holiness. The Redcrosse Knight and Una encounter Error, half serpent and half woman, in a forest-like setting, suggesting the Fall story. Yet, as E. Smith has pointed out,

> The historicity of a first fall is neither affirmed nor denied in any exclusive terms, and the state of the Red Cross Knight at the beginning is neither totally depraved nor totally paradisaic; Adam is not only the first man, but all men, of whom the Knight is one. (*Some Versions of the Fall*, 98–99)

If Spenser's self-consciously fictive epic treats its Adam figure somewhat ambiguously, a more straightforward rendering of the Fall story occurs in his 'Hymne of Heavenly Love':

> But man forgetfull of his makers grace,
> No lesse then Angels, whom he did ensew,
> Fell from the hope of promist heavenly place,
> Into the mouth of death to sinner dew,
> And all his off-spring into thraldome threw. (120–24)

Sir Walter Raleigh, a correspondent of Spenser, was certainly not setting up straw men when he spoke out against the tendency to read the Adam and Eve story as allegory. In his *History of the World* Raleigh lamented the Vulgate's rendering of Genesis 2:8 (*'Plantauerat Dominus Deus Paradisum voluptatis a principio'*), in which 'Eden' becomes *voluptatis* ('pleasure') and 'eastward' becomes *a principio* ('at the beginning') as an allegorical reading of a geographical passage. Eden, he wrote, is as much a part of world geography as 'that land west of Cuba that the Spaniards call Florida' and has similar meaning, 'pleasure or flourishing' (1.3.3).

Shakespeare used the Adam tradition almost entirely for secular, even comical, purposes. In *Much Ado About Nothing*, Beatrice and Benedick take turns evoking the Genesis story in unusual and humorous ways. First Beatrice vows that she will never marry:

> Not till God made men of some other metal than earth.
> Would it not grieve a woman to be overmaster'd with a piece
> of valiant dust? to make an account of her life to a clod of
> wayward marl? No, uncle, I'll none. Adam's sons are my
> brethren, and truly I hold it a sin to match in my kindred.
> (2.1.50–55)

Benedick, for his part, swears, 'I would not marry her though she were endowed with all that Adam had left before he transgressed' (2.1.218–20). In *Love's Labour's Lost* (5.2.323) Berowne observes of the witty and silver-tongued Boyet, 'Had he been Adam, he had tempted Eve'.

Elsewhere in Shakespeare the Adam image has more serious implications, as in the Henry trilogy, where repeated references to the 'old man' and 'th' offending Adam' (2 Henry 4; Henry 5, 5.1.1.28–29) underscore Falstaff's comic and pathetic identification: 'Dost thou hear, Hal? Thou knowest in the state of innocency Adam fell; and what should poor Jack Falstaff do in the days of villainy?' (Henry IV (1), 3.3.172–74).

Milton provides the most complete statement of the Adam tradition in world literature. Paradise Lost, according to its own declarations, is an epic apologia in the context of 17th-century culture. The poet invokes the Spirit to enable him 'to justifie the wayes of God to men' (1.26). The long description of the Satanic rebellion, specifically placed before the introduction of Adam, is designed to indicate that Adam's disobedience does not have God as its source. So, too, the visit of Raphael to prelapsarian Adam (books 5–8), surely a major portion of the poem, functions chiefly in the poem as rendering Adam without excuse. Milton previously has the Deity ensure that he is not held responsible either for Satan's fall (3.95ff.) or for Adam's (3.111ff.).

For Milton, Adam was created by the Son with only a single restriction: 'Not to taste that onely tree' (4.423). 'The rest, we live / Law to our selves, our Reason is our Law' (9.653–54). Seduced by the serpent, the woman eats of the forbidden fruit, and Adam follows her, though he is not deceived (10.145). Having enjoyed pure physical love before the Fall (4.312, 506), they now, immediately afterward, engage in an orgiastic union which marks their fallen nature. The poet seems to have sifted carefully through the various theological traditions of European culture to recover every detail and tradition which might aid him in his specifically apologetic cause.

Milton was responding to the secular forces which were calling into question – or even ridiculing – the whole notion of a historical Adam and a geographical Eden. In the burlesque Hudibras, by Samuel Butler, Milton's contemporary, it is said of the titular hero that he knew

... the seat of Paradise,
Could tell in what degree it lies;
And, as he was disposed, could prove it,
Below the moon, or else above it:
What Adam dreamt of when his bride,

Came from her closet in his side:
Whether the devil tempted her
By a High-Dutch interpreter;
If either of them had a navel;
Who first made music malleable;
Whether the serpent, at the fall,
Had cloven feet, or none at all. (1.173–84)

The satirical tone of Butler is all the more biting because his description reflects the actual concerns of his contemporary writers, such as Sir Thomas Browne, who alludes to the notion of original sin with the memorable words 'The man without a navel yet lives in me' (*Religio Medici*, 2.10) and in his *Pseudodoxia Epidemica* devotes a chapter to the 'error' of artists such as Michelangelo who represent the first man with a navel. Ironically, Milton's own use of the epic form contributed to the further decline of the Adam tradition. Increasingly, after Milton writers talk mythically of the Fall but not historically of Adam.

One of the most radical mythic departures from the biblical story is that of Blake, who inverted the vision of *Paradise Lost* to create his own version of the Fall in which

The Combats of Good and Evil is Eating of the Tree of Knowledge. The Combats of Truth and Error is Eating of the Tree of Life... There is not an Error but it has a Man for its Agent, that is, it is a Man. There is not Truth, but it has also a Man. (*A Vision of the Last Judgment*)

Lord Byron, too, employs the Fall story, but Adam is merely a minor character in his tragedy *Cain*, which centres on Adam's firstborn. Mary Shelley's classic *Frankenstein* echoes the biblical story with its implication that Frankenstein usurps the knowledge of God in the manner of Adam.

The protagonist of George Eliot's *Adam Bede* is a young carpenter who manages the woods of a great estate and whose character is torn between what he knows is moral on the one hand and what is attractive and immoral on the other. Robert Browning adopts the talmudic story of Lilith to present a very human Adam in a most unusual *ménage à trois*, in his 'Adam, Lilith, and Eve'.

In 20th-century literature, Adam is most often a completely mythical figure whom writers use to denote themes of societal conflict (e.g., Shaw's *Back to Methuselah* or Edwin Muir's 'Adam's Dream', in which the traditional story is applied to the confusion in modern life), or the common plight of mankind (Yeats, 'Adam's Curse' and 'Why Should Old Men Be Mad?'), or some aspect of the perceived conflict between the sexes (as in John Fowles' several novels), or a nostalgic longing for a golden youth (Dylan Thomas, 'Fern Hill'). The Adam figure has a more traditional role in G.K. Chesterton's 'In Praise of Dust' and C.S. Lewis' *Perelandra*.

American literature from the colonial period on has been characterized by a persistent attraction to the character and the narrative of Adam. Hawthorne and Melville, as well as Walt Whitman, James Fenimore Cooper, and Montgomery Bird, contributed to the literary development of the American Adam. No American writer, however, made greater use of the Adam tradition than Mark Twain. Not only did he write the delightful and witty *Extracts from Adam's Diary* (1893), which was reprinted with *Eve's Diary* (1905) in 1931 as *The Private Lives of Adam and Eve*, but he also used many of the significant themes of the Adam tradition in some of his better-known works such as *Huckleberry Finn*, where the images of the innocence of Adam's Edenic world are central to Huck's experiences.

Anthony D. York
University of Cincinnati

Cain

Cain, whose name in Hebrew means 'smith', was the eldest son of Adam and Eve. His story, related in Genesis 4:1–17, immediately follows the Fall, God's curses on the serpent, humankind, and the earth, and the expulsion of Adam and Eve from Eden (Genesis 3). The Cain narrative divides into two parts, murder and exile. The first part is a tale of sibling rivalry and fratricide, as Cain, 'tiller of the ground', slays his younger brother Abel, a shepherd, after the Lord accepts Abel's sacrificial offering but spurns Cain's. Following this murder Cain disavows his brother ('Am I my brother's keeper?' 4:9). The narrative is thematically related to the Fall and God's curses on Adam,

81

Eve, and the earth, since God explains to Cain that he shall be 'cursed from the earth' (4:11), and that when he tills the ground, 'it shall not henceforth yield unto thee her strength'. In the second part of the Cain story, God orders that Cain become 'a fugitive and a vagabond in the earth' (4:12). When Cain fears that he will be slain in his wanderings, God proclaims that he shall be avenged 'sevenfold' if anyone should kill him and places on him a 'mark' (4:15). Finally, Cain wanders to the land of Nod, 'on the east of Eden' (4:16), builds the world's first city, and names it Enoch after his son. The remainder of Genesis 4 chronicles Cain's descendants, including Lamech and his sons and daughter, who make various discoveries. The Cain narrative, then, represents a moralized tale of the continuing descent from Eden, the original garden, to the city and its luxuries. Passages in the New Testament connect Cain with Satan (1 John 3:12) and present him as an evil example (Jude 11).

English writers from the Renaissance to the 18th century invoked Cain's name especially as a curse. Marlowe's Barabas in *The Jew of Malta*, for example, characterizes Lodowicke as 'This offspring of Cain, this Jebusite' (2.3.301), while the newly crowned Henry IV, in Shakespeare's *Richard II*, banishes Exton, slayer of Richard, with the words: 'with Cain go wander through the shades of night' (5.6.43). Moreover, Claudius confesses that his 'offense is rank': 'It hath the primal eldest curse upon it, / A brother's murder' (*Hamlet*, 3.3.36–38). If medieval writers were fascinated by Cain as a historical figure of biblical primitivism, these later writers saw him rather as a byword, as the figural progenitor of a 'cursed' race (Donne's *Progresse of the Soule*, 516). Milton speaks of Cain as the 'sweaty Reaper' (*Paradise Lost*, 11.434) and reiterates the common view that his sacrifice was rejected because it was half-hearted; he likens Cain to Judas, who also despaired of God's grace (*De Doctrina Christiana*, 2.3). For Dryden, Cain is the archetype of violence and murder, a spirit 'latent' in Adam's seed which would lead ultimately to the religious divisions of Dryden's times (*The Hind and the Panther*, 1.279).

In the later 18th and early 19th century, writers began to reassess Cain's significance. If Christ brought about the possibility of salvation for all sinners, does this include the hardest cases such as

82

Cain, or Judas the despised suicide? Are these traitors to humankind and deity damned from the beginning? Influenced by Arminianism, particularly after translations of Salomon Gessner's sentimental *Der Tod Abels* (1758), English and American writers inquired as to Cain's state of mind and discovered a brother who came to hate his more successful sibling, a soul to be pitied, even a scapegoat or a human being in distress.

In Coleridge's *The Wanderings of Cain* (1798) Abel's ghost returns to torment Cain while he and his young son wander by moonlight in the wilderness. Enos pathetically asks his father why the squirrels refuse to play with him. A man of poetic imagination, Cain replies: 'The Mighty One that persecuteth me is on this side and on that; / he pursueth my soul like the wind, like the sand-blast he passeth through me; / he is around me even as the air!' (31–33).

Byron, in his drama *Cain: A Mystery* (1821), exploits the moral and psychological complexities of Cain's dilemma. A man who 'thirst[s] for good' (2.2.238) but who is preoccupied with death, Cain recognizes the world's beauty and sadness, but from the play's opening he feels cut off from his family, even from his sister-wife Adah. When Lucifer observes that the world before the Fall was lovely, Cain realizes that his quarrel is not with the still beautiful earth but with his own restless unhappiness:

> It is not with the earth, though I must till it,
> I feel at war, but that I may not profit
> By what it bears of beautiful, untoiling,
> Nor gratify my thousand swelling thoughts
> With knowledge, nor allay my thousand fears
> Of death and life. (2.2.124–30)

Cain bitterly criticizes his parents for depriving him of his inheritance, Eden, and for preferring Abel to him, a resentment Lucifer manipulates. Lucifer imparts to Cain Faustian knowledge, including a vision of Hades and the 'mighty Pre-Adamites'; and Cain, like some primeval Wordsworth, equates his son's infancy with lost innocence (3.1.18–34). After the murder Eve delivers a terrible curse on her firstborn, banishing him from the Adamic fellowship.

William Blake answered Coleridge and Byron in *The Ghost of*

Abel (1822), in which Abel returns to denounce the Lord and stir up revenge: 'My desire is unto Cain', says the Ghost, 'And He doth rule over Me' (31–32). In this poetic drama Blake challenges the implicit Byronic equation of criminality and the visionary imagination. Cain has typically been romanticized in the modern period; he becomes the visionary wanderer, estranged from ordinary society, both cursed and privileged with a terrible burden of guilt. Here is the informing principle of not only the Wandering Jew, the Ancient Mariner, and Shelley's *Adonais*, but also Melville's Ishmael, Twain's Huck Finn, Conrad's Lord Jim, Steinbeck's Cal (*East of Eden*), Kerouac's Dean Moriarty (*On the Road*), and John Gardner's *Grendel*. In J.W. Thompson's *Cain* (1926), the original fratricide is a heroic figure who has 'something of the character of Prometheus, something of that of Milton's Satan' (page 6).

James M. Dean
University of Delaware

Esau

The narrative concerning Esau (Genesis 25–28) is inseparable from that of his twin brother Jacob and the story of the lost birthright. The salient features of Esau's characterization for later literary development are that he was a hunter (25:27), was red and hirsute (27:11), and sold his birthright as eldest son to his twin for a mess of red pottage (25:30). He was thus named Edom (red), and he became father of the Edomites (cf. Genesis 36:1).

Esau has been much overshadowed in literature by his brother, the relative richness of theological reflection and symbol notwithstanding. Milton, in 'Eikonoklastes', allows him to be a figure for the Presbyterians (Jacob stands for the independent Puritans); Melville refers to the rarity of twin births in whales with an allusion to the story in *Moby Dick*. A more favourable reference comes in a letter to John Hamilton Reynolds from Keats, who wonders why modern poets should be so limited as Wordsworth and Hunt 'when we can wander with Esau'. 'Wandering about in the east' is made by Galsworthy to reflect 'the curse of Esau' (*Flowering Wilderness*, chapter 1), however, and in *The Way of all Flesh* Butler writes that Ernest's marriage to Ellen, his mother's maid, was worse than his 'marriage' to the Church: 'He was an Esau – one of those wretches whose hearts the Lord has hardened'. In Rudy Wiebe's chapter 'Sons and Heirs' in *The Blue Mountains of China*, Escha is a red-haired Russian serf whom his putative Mennonite half-brother Jacob kills after a drunken sexual initiation in the ruins of Jacob's Gnadenfeld *hof*.

Ironically empathetic is A.M. Klein, who, in a reflection on the persecution of the Jews in his 'Childe Harold's Pilgrimage', parodies a sympathy of Byron's when he makes 'Esau, my kinsman' a man who would 'devise a different answer for the foe; / And let the argumentative bullet dent / The heart of the tyrant, let the steel blade show' – an option not so morally available to the son of Jacob who receives the Torah: 'Alas for me that in my ears there sounds / Always the sixth thunder of Sinai.'

David L. Jeffrey
University of Ottawa

Eve

The Bible says that while Adam slept, God created Eve from one of Adam's ribs to be a 'help meet for him'; at first the text refers to her simply as 'woman' (Genesis 2:20–22), thereby establishing her generic relationship to all women as well as her genetic relationship to man: 'Adam said... she shall be called Woman, because she was taken out of Man' (2:23). The author then states her normative marital relationship to the man – 'they shall be one flesh' (2:24) – and outlines her encounter with the serpent (involving, first, credulity, 3:1–6, but afterwards, according to the so-called 'protevangelium' of 3:15, enmity). It is only after this account of humankind's creation, disobedience, and judgment that Adam is said to call his wife by a proper name: 'Adam called his wife's name Eve; because she was the mother of all living' – *mater viventium* (Vulgate, Genesis 3:20). Her name thus bespeaks her role as life-giver, a role emphasized by the Old Testament's second and last mention of her name: 'Adam knew Eve his wife; and she conceived, and bare Cain' (Genesis 4:1). Eve, then, both participates in the sin of disobeying God and signifies the gift of continuing generational life. One of the two New Testament

85

references to her reinforces these negative and positive functions. St Paul comments, 'Adam was first formed, then Eve. And Adam was not deceived, but the woman being deceived was in the transgression. Notwithstanding she [i.e., a woman] shall be saved in childbearing' (1 Timothy 2:13–15). The other New Testament reference to her, also by Paul, presents her, beguiled by the serpent, as one whose example the church ought not to follow (2 Corinthians 11:3). Yet here too the negative associations pertaining to Eve exist side by side with the positive, for Paul also implicitly compares her to the Corinthian church, which he wishes to present 'as a chaste virgin to Christ' (2 Corinthians 11:2; cf. Ephesians 5:22–27).

The richest and fullest treatment of Eve in English is Milton's. Within the context of the theodicy of *Paradise Lost* (1667), Milton recognizes that an 'unfallen' Eve actually possessing the faults ascribed to her by Raleigh, Peyton, and others would stand as an indictment of the justice and providence of her creator. Thus Milton takes pains to depict her as both conspicuously fallible – for how else could human free agency meaningfully have operated? – and yet decidedly unfallen. And her unfallen marriage with Adam involves full intercourse, both sexual and intellectual, in accordance with Milton's conviction that the blessings of marriage are not to be viewed as either entailing or resulting from the Fall and that 'there is a peculiar comfort in the married state besides the genial bed, which no other society affords' (*Tetrachordon*, 1645, in *Complete Prose Works*, 1953–82, 2.596). As Diane McColley puts it, 'while retaining some degree of subordination for Eve, [Milton in *Paradise Lost*] purges that state of all suggestion of weakness or wickedness, inferiority or limitation, carnal precedence or unequal responsibility, and avoids the radically false dichotomy of opposing freedom and service' (*Milton's Eve*, 35).

Paradise Lost forms the principal backdrop for many subsequent treatments of Eve in English. Dryden's Eve, like Milton's, has full sexual relations with Adam before the Fall, though Dryden trivializes that aspect of their marriage: in Act 2, Scene 1 of *The State of Innocence and Fall of Man* (1712), the supposedly prelapsarian Eve, sounding a little like Chaucer's Wife of Bath, implies a connection between the withholding or granting of sexual favours and the maintenance or loss of her 'much lov'd Soveraignty'. Eve appears in Blake's late vision *The*

Ghost of Abel (1822) as well as in Byron's drama *Cain* (1821), in which she utters a long and vehement curse against her Byronic firstborn. Elsewhere, Byron frequently alludes to the sexual associations of Eve, though he assumes, unlike Dryden and Milton, that life before the Fall was sexless and boring (e.g., *Don Juan*, 1.18), an opinion which has increasingly taken hold in thought and literature since the Romantic period. Visual depictions of Eve are discussed in Robert Browning's 'Parleyings with Francis Furini', in which one of the issues is the interrelationship of art and lust (157, 180). And Eve's relationship to her offspring is a main theme of Elizabeth Barrett Browning's *A Drama of Exile*. This play, focusing on the postlapsarian scene, develops Milton's portrayal of the magnanimous and penitent Eve. Christ himself, whom Eve addresses as 'Seed' (1754), appears and commands Adam to 'bless the woman'; and Adam, obeying, honours Eve as 'First woman, wife, and mother!... / And also the sole bearer of the Seed / Whereby sin dieth' (1837–39). The maternal and loving characteristics of Eve receive further emphasis in Christina Rossetti's 'Eve' (1865), a lament Eve utters after the murder of Abel, though in this poem, as the occasion would suggest, the tone of the reference to Eve as *mater viventium* is much more sombre than it is in Elizabeth Browning's exploration of the protevangelium: Rossetti's Eve exclaims, 'I, Eve, sad mother / Of all who must live' (26–27).

In the 20th century the theme of Eve as *mater viventium* is given a new twist by the Irish writer James Stephens. In his poem 'Eve' (in *The Hill of Vision*, 1912, 100–103), Eve precedes Adam; indeed, she gives birth to him, after she has felt 'Immensity's caress' and the 'primal kiss'. In this way Eve is removed from her traditional narrative context and made to embody a primal and eternal feminine principle. G.B. Shaw similarly removes Eve from the bounds of time. In *Back to Methuselah*, Eve does appear at the beginning of history but reappears far on in time, in AD31,920, and together with Adam and Cain has an opportunity to evaluate history, once (in Cain's words) 'the strong have slain one another; and the weak live for ever'. And although Adam can make 'nothing of it', it is Eve who declares, 'All's well'.

In 20th-century American writing, Eve's presence is the subject of Robert Frost's beautiful sonnet 'Never Again Would Birds' Song Be the Same', which portrays Adam's wonder at how the voice of the newly created Eve has somehow infused nature itself with a new richness. By contrast, Archibald MacLeish, in *Songs for Eve* (1954, in *New and Collected Poems, 1917–1976*, 1976), glorifies Eve's sin as a kind of Byronic rebellion, seeing the unfallen state as tedious and insipid and, hence, disobedience to God as an act of transcendence: 'But for [Eve's] fault the wine / Were sweet as water is' ('What the Vine Said to Eve'). Similarly, for MacLeish, the savour of sex required the consciousness which came with the Fall; as Eve puts it, Adam 'touched me never till he took / The apple from my hand' ('Eve in Dawn'). *The Book of Eve* (1973), a novel by Canadian writer Constance Beresford-Howe, suggests too that Eve's 'fall' was guiltless and liberating. Its protagonist, Eva, a modern though ageing woman, leaves her home and her husband to make a fresh start in life.

Dennis Danielson
University of British Columbia

Hagar

Hagar was the handmaiden of Sarah (Genesis 16–17; 21) who, when Sarah proved unable to bear children for her husband Abraham, was presented to him in order that Sarah might have a child by a surrogate. The resulting male child was named Ishmael. Some years afterward came an extraordinary promise to Abraham, the beginning of the covenant, whereby Abraham was promised an heir, through Sarah, in his old age. After Sarah's son Isaac was born, rivalry between the two women grew so intense that Abraham was persuaded to exile Hagar and Ishmael into the desert. The Genesis story is concerned with God's preservation of Hagar and her offspring, while making it clear that his covenantal blessing resided with the second son, the offspring of Sarah.

Christian typological reading of the story begins in Galatians 4:22–27. Here St Paul describes the Genesis account as an allegory, which he reads as follows: 'for these are the two covenants; the one from the mount Sinai, which gendereth to bondage, which is Agar. For this Agar is mount Sinai in Arabia, and answereth to Jerusalem which now is, and is in bondage with her children. But Jerusalem which is above is free, which is the mother of us all' (4:24b–26).

In literary characterization within the Christian tradition of the Middle Ages and the Renaissance, Hagar figures only indirectly, usually as an image of the outcast and rebel. In Shakespeare's *Merchant of Venice* ('What says that fool of Hagar's offspring, ha?' [2.5.44]), the perspective is 'old law' and the allusion is therefore culturally reversed, to a Gentile. Milton's Satan implies, as he commences his temptation of Christ, that the latter's desert condition is like that of Hagar and Ishmael (*Paradise Regained*, 2.308). In an essay of Daniel Defoe in *The Review* (no. 3, 15 September 1711), he develops the theme of Hagar's prayer, 'give me not poverty, lest I steal', to make the point that economic 'distress removes from the soul... all obligations moral or religious'. Moll Flanders, Roxanna, and Captain Jack among his outcast protagonists all claim Hagar's predicament and excuse. But even with inversions, the covenantal connection remains: Coleridge's Zapolya will comfort herself and her child, saying, 'Thou art no Hagar's offspring: thou art the rightful heir to an appointed king' (*Zapolya*, 1.1.439), appealing in her case to the Pauline identification. Blake anticipates modern feeling, however, and puts Hagar and Ishmael back with Abraham, Sarah, and Isaac in *The Last Judgment*.

In the modern period Hagar herself figures more directly in English literature. Aside from her use in incidental allusion, she becomes heroine to a spate of quasi-historical fictions written in America during the 19th and 20th century, which for the most part concern either the ironies of divine judgment or the romance of rejection. *Hagar*, by Pearl Rivers (Mrs Elizabeth Poitrevant), *Hagar in the Wilderness* by Nathaniel Parker Willis, and *Hagar's Farewell* by Augusta Moore are exemplary of the wide appeal of the outcast handmaiden in the United States during the 1920s and 1930s.

The Stone Angel (1964), a novel by Canadian author Margaret Laurence, takes the modern tradition a step further. Here, the heroine is called Hagar and her husband Bram, but the novel seeks to explore the psychology of the Pauline exegesis from the outcast side, in a characterization of the rebellious spirit facing death, utterly defiant of repentance.

Camille R. La Bossière
University of Ottawa

Isaac

Isaac (in Hebrew, 'he laughs') was the second of the patriarchs of Israel, the only son of Abraham and Sarah, husband of Rebecca, and the father of Esau and Jacob. His name is connected with Sarah's immediate response to the divine promise that she would bear a son though long past childbearing age – she found the notion risible (Genesis 18:12–15) – and with the laughter at once comic and joyful which followed the realization of that promise (Genesis 21:6). Genesis 22 relates what became for posterity the most significant episode in the life of Isaac, Abraham's offering of his obedient son at God's command. As he approaches his death, old and blind, Isaac is victim again, though of a different kind, in his deception at the hands of Rebecca and Jacob, who conspire to strip Esau of his birthright (Genesis 27). The New Testament recalls Abraham's offering of Isaac as an example of faith (Hebrews 11:17) and obedience (James 2:21).

The Fathers of the Church read in Abraham's offering of Isaac a type of the crucifixion and a prefiguration of the eucharist: the sacrifice of the son by the father foreshadowed God's willingness to offer his only begotten son for the redemption of mankind. Structured in accordance with this typology, medieval plays of Abraham and Isaac are comedies centred not on the father but on the son. The typology which generates the medieval comedies of Abraham and Isaac is altogether absent from Theodore Beza's *Abraham Sacrifiant* (*A Tragedie of Abrahams Sacrifice*, translated by Arthur Golding, 1577). In this Protestant classical tragedy, the protagonist, a man and no more, is confronted with the awesome choice between two horrifying alternatives – killing his son or disobeying his God. A 'witty comedy or interlude' in five acts, the anonymous *History of Jacob and Esau* (1568) casts Isaac in the role of a pious and kindly father who accepts God's will in all things. He comes to love Esau all the more for having forgiven Jacob his trickery and having accepted the lot accorded him by heaven's king.

Henry Vaughan considers Isaac's marriage in his poem of that title, which takes as its text Genesis 24:63 ('And Isaac went out to pray [King James Version 'meditate'] in the field at eventide'). This verse was frequently alluded to in Renaissance discussions of meditation (cf. *Pilgrim's Progress*, which opens with Christian walking 'solitarily in the fields, sometimes reading, and sometimes praying: and thus… he spent his time'). George Herbert infers from the case of Abraham and Isaac that 'the godly are exempt from Law', but not from obeying God's will (*Briefe Notes on Valdesso's Considerations*, 62). For Richard Crashaw in '*Lauda Sion Salvatorem*', both Isaac and the ram sacrificed in his stead prefigure Christ in the eucharist (stanza 12). Abraham Cowley's *Davideis* is more domestic, imagining the feelings of 'the sad old Man' and 'the inn'ocent Boy' as they approach the moment of sacrifice, then picturing the child's exuberant response to his release (300–328). For Sir Thomas Browne in *Religio Medici*, the appearance of the ram at just the right moment illustrates how mysterious the ways of providence really are (1.15).

Walter Scott's Isaac of York in *Ivanhoe* suggests something of his biblical namesake: the sound of a bugle rescues him at the last moment from death by fire. In the 'Genesis' chapter of *Sartor Resartus*, Carlyle seems to parody the Bible's account of Isaac's miraculous entry into the world (2.1). The reference in Thomas Hardy's *Tess of the D'Urbervilles*, by contrast, is direct and charged with pathos: Mr Clare mourns over his son Angel 'as Abraham might have mourned over the doomed Isaac while they went up the hill together' (chapter 49).

James Joyce's *Finnegans Wake* plays with the second patriarch of Israel, his name and life. 'A bland old Isaac', who is 'buttended' by a 'kidscad' on the first page, is subsequently victimized by a running joke on butting, ramming, and asses. In the short story 'England, My England', D.H. Lawrence is earnest: the Catholic patriarch Godfrey Marshall 'was a man who kept alive the old red flame of fatherhood, fatherhood that had even the right to sacrifice the child to God, like Isaac'.

David L. Jeffrey
University of Ottawa

Ishmael

Ishmael was the natural son of Abraham and Hagar, the handmaiden of Abraham's wife Sarah. He was conceived after Sarah had herself proved unable to produce a child. After Ishmael's conception Hagar became contemptuous of her mistress, and consequently fled into the wilderness. There an angel of the Lord appeared to comfort her (Genesis 16:11) and directed her to return and submit to Sarah.

In the Genesis 21 account Hagar and her son were sent into the desert by Sarah, who saw Ishmael as a threat to her own son Isaac, more recently born to her after many years of barrenness. The angel of God told both Abraham and Hagar (21:12–13, 17–18) that Ishmael would be the founder of a mighty nation; the Ishmaelites subsequently became the enemy of God's chosen people (Psalm 83:6).

In Galatians 4:22–31, St Paul discusses the story of Ishmael and Hagar as an 'allegory' which differentiates between the two covenants: 'the one from the mount Sinai, which gendereth to bondage, which is Agar... But Jerusalem which is above is free, which is the mother of us all... Now we, brethren, as Isaac was, are the children of promise... We are not children of the bondwoman, but of the free.'

References to Ishmael in English literature are diverse. Spenser's *Faerie Queene* (3.3.6.7) refers to 'the Africk Ismaell', evoking Ishmael's associations with the Arabs and Saracens. In Shakespeare's *The Merchant of Venice*, Shylock, one of God's chosen people, finds himself ironically in the position of Ishmael, an outcast in a society which is largely composed of 'Hagar's offspring' (2.5.44), or Gentiles. In *Paradise Regained* (2.306–310), Satan tempts Jesus, hungry after his long fast, with a reference to the son of the 'Fugitive Bondwoman', who would have perished in the desert had he not 'found... relief by a providing Angel' (cf. Genesis 31:17–19).

Henry Vaughan in some of his poems reflects an interpretation of the story in which Ishmael becomes a type of the Gentiles, latter-day heirs of the promise; God's providential preservation of him foreshadows his grace bestowed on suppliant believers: 'If pious griefs Heavens joys awake / O fill his bottle! Thy childe weeps!' ('The Seed Growing Secretly'; cf. 'Providence', 'Begging', 'The Timber').

William Blake, in *A Vision of the Last Judgment*, includes Ishmael along with Abraham, Sarah, and Isaac in part of the community of the Just. But Coleridge, in *Zapolya*, uses the image of Hagar and Ishmael to denote exile and alienation. Ironically, Zapolya and her child, 'the rightful heir' (*Zapolya*, 1.1.440), are treated in much the way Hagar

Didst flye, whose children wrought thy childrens wo:
Yet thou in all thy solitude and grief,
On stones didst sleep and found'st but cold relief;
Thou from the Day-star a long way didst stand
And all that distance was Law and command.
But we a healing Sun by day and night,
Have our sure Guardian, and our leading light;
What thou didst hope for and believe, we finde
And feel a friend most ready, sure and kinde.
Thy pillow was but type and shade at best,
But we the substance have, and on him rest.

Enlightenment poetry is on the whole less favourable to Jacob. Dryden's political allegorizing of 'Jacob's seed... chosen to rebel' (*Absalom and Achitophel*, 2.6) concentrates on his descendants, finding in many of them Jacob's vices (1.977–84; cf. 'To Sir Godfrey Kneller', 93–96). In 'Sandys' Ghost' Pope hears 'the Beat of Jacob's Drums. / Poor Ovid finds no Quarter!' a reference to what Pope sees as overuse of Old Testament allusion in literature. While William Blake's admiration for stories of usurpation is extensive, Jacob becomes an analogue of fallen Adam, with Esau or Edom a type of Adam in innocence and restored: 'Now is the dominion of Edom, & the return of Adam into Paradise' ('The Marriage of Heaven and Hell', pl. 3). For Robert Browning, 'Smooth Jacob still robs homely Esau: / Now up, now down, the world's one see-saw' ('The Flight of the Duchess', 907–908).

The account of Jacob wrestling with the angel at the ford of the River Jabbok is replete with Hebrew puns (Genesis 32:24–32). Several of these relate to the root of Jacob's name, and its compound standing as a west Semitic diminutive of 'The Lord will pursue' or 'The Lord preserves'. At the River Jabbok, Jacob confronted a great question: Would he cross back over as he came the first time, on the strength of his own staff (32:10)? Or would he, as John Donne puts it in a sermon (ed. Potter and Simpson, 1.7), learn to proceed in the strength of God's elective will for him? Apprehensive about the reception he was to receive from his wronged brother Esau, he sent a conciliatory message and a lavish present ahead and waited alone at the ford of the river, where 'there wrestled a man with him until the breaking of the day'.

When Jacob's opponent 'saw that he prevailed not against him, he touched the hollow of his thigh... and he said, "Let me go, for the day breaketh."' The man who had more or less lived by 'blows below the belt' now received one. Yet Jacob, who had wrestled also with his twin in the womb and for whom striving was characteristic, persevered, saying, 'I will not let thee go, except thou bless me'. Although the mysterious opponent did not comply with Jacob's request that he reveal his name (v. 29), Jacob obtained the coveted blessing, which was confirmed in a transformation of his own name: 'Thy name shall be called no more Jacob ('crooked') but Israel' (possibly 'God is reliable'). Jacob then named the place Peniel ('appearance of God' or 'face of God'), 'for he said, I have seen God face to face, and my life is preserved' (32:30).

The most famous poem of Charles Wesley, admired by Isaac Watts and others as one of the great achievements of religious verse in its time, is his 'Wrestling Jacob'. Combining insights from Luther and Augustine, Wesley concentrates on the 'confession' of Jacob to the angel and his conversion to 'Israel'. The transformation models that of any Christian pilgrim coming to grips with the divine antagonist who, though perhaps at first seeming merely a mysterious stranger or a 'Traveller unknown', reveals himself at last as 'Jesus, the feeble sinner's friend'. Wesley juxtaposes the Genesis text with a citation from Hosea 12:4, as if applied to the daybreak revelation after a long, dark night of the soul:

> The Sun of Righteousness on me
> Hath rose with healing in his wings:
> Withered my nature's strength; from thee
> My soul its life and succour brings.
> My help is all laid up above:
> Thy nature and thy name is Love.
> Contented now, upon my thigh
> I halt, till life's short journey end;
> All helplessness, all weakness, I
> On thee alone for strength depend...

Christina Rossetti interpolates a reference to the Song of Solomon (2:10) in her treatment of the passage:

> Weeping we hold him fast to-night;
> We will not let Him go
> Till daybreak smite our wearied sight
> And summer smile the snow.
> Then figs shall bud, and dove with dove
> Shall coo the livelong day;
> Then He shall say 'Arise, My love,
> My fair one, come away'. (cf. Matthew 24:30–32)

In Aubray de Vere's 'Jerusalem', it is the City of David which bears the eponymous character of the event, as Israel before a God who looks upon that history and 'knows that thou, obscured and dim, / Thus wrestling all night long with him, / Shalt victor rise at last'.

In American literature many references are secularized and imprecise. The angel figures as Art, and the artist has 'Jacob's mystic heart' in Melville's *Timoleon*; Emily Dickinson has the wrestling match take place 'A little over Jordan', and whimsically notes:

> The Angel begged permission
> To breakfast and return.
>
> 'Not so', quoth wily Jacob,
> And girt his loins anew,
> 'Until thou bless me, stranger!'
> The which acceded to:
>
> Light swung the silver fleeces
> Peniel hills among
> And the astonished Wrestler
> Found he had worsted God!

The narrator in Hawthorne's *The House of Seven Gables* observes that 'a recluse, like Hepzibah, usually displays remarkable frankness, and at least temporary affability, on being absolutely cornered and brought to the point of personal intercourse; – like the angel whom Jacob wrestled with, she is ready to bless you, when once overcome'. In

Longfellow's *Evangeline*, 'wild with the winds of September / Wrestled the trees of the forest, as Jacob / of old with the angel' (1.2). Whittier, in *My Soul and I*, advises:

> The Present, the Present is all thou hast
> For thy sure possessing;
> Like the patriarch's angel hold it fast
> Till it gives its blessing.

The wrestling can also become a figure for a modern 'dark night of the soul', as in Howells' *The Rise of Silas Lapham*:

> He went in and shut the door, and by and by his wife heard him begin walking up and down. But when the first light whitened the window, the words of the Scripture came into her mind: 'And there wrestled a man with him until the breaking of the day... And he said, "Let me go, for the day breaketh." And he said, "I will not let thee go, except thou bless me"'. (chapter 25)

Similarly, Doña Maria 'wrestled with the ghost of her temptation and was worsted on every occasion' in Thornton Wilder's *The Bridge of San Luis Rey* (chapter 2), and both psychological torment and sexual implications may lie behind Hemingway's use of 'Jacob' as his struggling protagonist in *The Sun Also Rises*. It is a sexual analogy exclusively which prompts Pat Lowther's 'Wrestling':

> Lover I must
> approach you as Jacob
> to his angel
> rough with that need.
> Yes I will
> pin you down,
> force answers from you. (*A Stone Diary*, 1977, 47)

A more generic development of the allusion occurs in Margaret Laurence's *Stone Angel*, in which the toppled marble angel marking her mother's grave is righted with difficulty by Hagar Shipley's son John; looking on, she wishes in vain he 'could have looked like Jacob then, wrestling with the angel and besting it, wringing a blessing from it with his might. But no' (chapter 6). Hagar's other son, Marvin, more faithful but less loved, comes to her on her deathbed, pleading for acknowledgment, and she reflects, 'Now it seems to me he is truly Jacob, gripping with all his strength and bargaining. I will not let thee go except thou bless me'. Hagar, who through a bitter life has herself become a 'stone angel', ponders: 'And I see I am thus strangely cast, and perhaps have been so from the beginning, and can only release myself by releasing him' (chapter 10).

David L. Jeffrey
University of Ottawa

Joseph

The story of Joseph, Jacob's favourite son, who was sold into slavery by his jealous brothers and ultimately rose to a position of prestige and prominence in Egypt, constitutes the entire final section of the book of Genesis. It is a masterpiece of biblical narrative, not only in its subtle characterization but also in its remarkable structural integrity. Joseph's first experiences with his family in Canaan and his later adventures and misadventures in Egypt – notably the attempted seduction by Potiphar's wife and his several demonstrations of remarkable skill as an interpreter of dreams – are woven together into a 'romance' plot which plays a pivotal role in the larger epic of Israel. The relocation of Joseph's father and brothers to Egypt, with which the narrative concludes, provides a sense of closure to Joseph's own quest for familial reunion and restoration and sets the stage for the great events of the Mosaic era: exile, exodus, wandering, and the receiving of the Law.

Surprisingly, the story of Joseph goes virtually unmentioned in the rest of the Bible. 'The tribe of Joseph' (i.e., the half-tribes of Ephraim and Manasseh) is referred to frequently in the Old Testament (and twice in the New Testament), but Joseph himself is spoken of only in the covenantal history of Psalm 105 (vv. 16–23). The Apocrypha is only slightly more attentive, with a few scattered references: Wisdom of Solomon 10:13–14 argues that Wisdom preserved Joseph in his Egyptian trials, and in 1 Maccabees 2:53 the dying Mattathias holds Joseph up to his sons as an example of one who kept the commandments of God under great duress. There is extensive treatment of Joseph in an ancient noncanonical romance now known as *Joseph and Asenath*, in which Joseph is portrayed in heroic terms and credited with angelic beauty. Joseph and his story are not mentioned at all in the New Testament.

Important for the literary tradition is the persistent identification of Joseph as a type of Christ. St Justin Martyr treats him in this way, as do Tertullian and St Irenaeus. Of special note also are the references scattered throughout the writings of St John Chrysostom (see especially his homily on Genesis 37, *Patrologia Graeca*, 54.528) and the complete book devoted to Joseph by St Ambrose (*De Joseph patriarchia*). In the latter text, Ambrose provides point-by-point correspondences between the lives of Joseph and Christ: Joseph suffered at the hands of his brothers; Jesus, at the hands of his people; Judah sold Joseph; Judas sold Jesus; Joseph, after revealing himself to his brothers, told them not to grieve (Genesis 45:5); and Jesus, after his resurrection, told his disciples not to fear (Matthew 28:10); Joseph's wife Asenath prefigured the church, the bride of Christ (*Patrologia Latina*, 14.646).

Typological patterns established by the Fathers find their way into all forms of medieval art: thus, for example, stained-glass windows at King's College, Cambridge, juxtapose Joseph's being cast into a well by his brothers with Christ's entombment and Reuben's seeking Joseph with the women's seeking the resurrected Christ. The same consistency may be found in the history of interpretation of individual episodes. An early tradition that Joseph's 'coat of many colours' (King James Version; the Revised Standard Version reads 'a long robe with sleeves') represents the humanity (and the mortal suffering) which Christ 'put on' in the incarnation may be found in the Old English poem *Physiologus*. This identification is reflected in medieval glossed Bibles (the *Glossa Ordinaria* and the *Bibles moralisées*) and in poems such as George Herbert's 'Joseph's Coat'. Herbert's poem makes no mention of Joseph except in the title, instead describing the identification of a believer's sufferings with those of Christ; the author assumes that the typological connections will be evident to the educated reader. In a transmuted form, that typology survives even in Blake, who has Joseph sold into slavery as an infant

– in order to emphasize continuity with Moses in the bulrushes and the flight of the Holy Family into Egypt – and suggests that the coat was a kind of swaddling-cloth complete with hieroglyphic stitching; he refers to Joseph 'stolen from his nurses cradle wrapd in needle-work / Of emblematic texture' (*Milton*, pl. 24, lines 18–19). In *Jerusalem* the reference to 'Josephs beautiful integument' (pl. 81, line 11) is given precisely the same typological context.

The identification of Joseph with Christ is sometimes so close that the two stories become entangled. In Melville's *Billy Budd*, the title character is evidently and persistently portrayed as a Christ figure, yet it is said of Claggart, when he has falsely accused Billy, that he surveys Captain Vere's face with 'a look that might have been that of the spokesman of the envious children of Jacob deceptively imposing on the troubled patriarch the blood-dyed coat of young Joseph'.

Joseph was a popular subject of Renaissance drama, both in England and abroad. English plays share with their continental counterparts an emphasis on the Egyptian scenes, as the titles of such plays as *Pharaoh's Favourite* (Robert Aylet, 1623) and *Egypt's Favourite* (Sir Francis Hubert, 1631) indicate. The Puritan ban on drama put an end to such entertainments, and Joseph's story did not find a significant place on the English stage again until the 18th century, with the production of Handel's highly operatic oratorio *Joseph* (1743). One year earlier, Henry Fielding created in Joseph Andrews, the titular character of one of his most popular novels, a chaste hero modelled to a considerable extent on his biblical namesake.

There have been few modern retellings in English of the Joseph narrative apart from minor sacred dramas and Webber and Rice's rock cantata *Joseph and the Amazing Technicolor Dreamcoat*. The definitive modern rendering of the Joseph story is Thomas Mann's magisterial four-volume series *Joseph and His Brothers*, published in Germany from 1933 to 1944 and translated into English in 1949. Mann's tetralogy – which finds its germ in Goethe's remark (in his autobiography *Dichtung und Wahrheit* [*Poetry and Truth*]) that the Joseph story is fascinating but 'thin' – reflects profound study of the whole range of Jewish and Christian interpretation, as well as an intimate knowledge of cultural anthropology and ancient history. It constitutes perhaps the greatest single commentary on the life of the biblical Joseph.

Allusions to individual episodes of the story are numerous in English literature. Joseph's famous chastity is earnestly invoked by Chaucer's Parson, who argues that the adulterous behaviour of Potiphar's wife exemplifies 'the fouleste thefte that may be, whan a womman steleth hir body from his housbonde' and that the wise Joseph 'of this thefte douted gretly' (*Parson's Tale*, 10.877–79). By the 19th century, that chastity could become a source of irony – as in Byron's *Don Juan* (1.187), when Juan is discovered in his lover Julia's closet by her husband, Alfonso:

> At last, as they more faintly wrestling lay,
> Juan contrived to give an awkward blow,
> And then his only garment quite gave way;
> He fled, like Joseph, leaving it; but there,
> I doubt, all likeness ends between the pair.

The same episode is sometimes invoked metaphorically, as in Emerson's 'Self-Reliance', where he urges his readers to 'leave your theory, as Joseph his coat in the hand of the harlot, and flee' (265).

Many writers recall Joseph's success in interpreting dreams; in Chaucer's *The Nun's Priest's Tale*, Chauntecleer cites Joseph's experience as proof that dreams do betoken truth; and in *The Book of the Duchess*, when the insomniac narrator finally falls asleep, he dreams a dream which, he asserts, even Joseph could not interpret (274–83). Even specific dreams recorded in the Genesis account have enriched our language and literature; thus Falstaff replies to Hal, who has just called him a 'stuffed cloak-bag of guts', by saying, 'If fat is to be hated, then Pharaoh's lean kine are to be loved' (*Henry IV (1)*, 2.4.414; cf. Genesis 41).

Alan Jacobs
Wheaton College

Noah

Noah is the central figure in two Old Testament narratives. As a 'just man' he, with his family, is preserved from annihilation in the flood (Genesis 6:5 – 9:17). As a cultural hero who discovers the art of making wine, he is surprised drunk by his son Ham; Noah later curses

Ham's son Canaan and blesses his own sons Shem and Japheth for respecting his shame (Genesis 9:25–27). Noah is the last of the antediluvian patriarchs and at the same time another Adam from whom mankind descends.

The meaning of the name *Noah* is not clear. In Genesis 5:29 the name is explained by a play on the Hebrew for 'to comfort', possibly a reference to the fact that the wine discovered by Noah was a source of consolation (Genesis 5:29). Some commentators and the Septuagint relate the name to the Hebrew word meaning 'to rest'. Noah is mentioned in the genealogies of 1 Chronicles 1:4 and Luke 3:38; he is called a righteous man (Ezekiel 14:14, 20) and a preacher of righteousness (2 Peter 2:5), and he is cited as an example of faith (Hebrews 11:7). Noah receives considerable attention in the Pseudepigrapha.

A parodic Noah figure appears in Chaucer's *Miller's Tale* in the character of an Oxford carpenter who fears a second flood. Shakespeare's Sir Toby refers to Noah the sailor in a comic context (*Twelfth Night*, 3.2.18–19). Drayton's *Noah's Flood* shows the protagonist in the role of preacher, as does Milton (*Paradise Lost*, 11.719–26), who regards Noah as the antitype of Adam (12.6–7) and type of the Christ to come (11.808–809, 876–77). In 'The Bunch of Grapes' George Herbert sees in Noah's vine a prefiguration of Christ 'who of the Laws sowre juice sweet wine did make, / Ev'n God himself being pressed for my sake' (cf. John 15:1). Marvell compares Cromwell, who 'planted the vine of liberty', to Noah and the Puritan opponents of Cromwell to Ham ('The First Anniversary of the Government'). For Dryden, Charles II rather than Cromwell is the Noah figure ('To His Sacred Majesty').

In the 17th, 18th and 19th centuries Noah is still occasionally invoked as a type of Christ (e.g., Keble, *The Christian Year*; Isaac Williams, *The Cathedral*; Francis Thompson, 'The Mistress of Vision'). More frequently, however, he is relegated to trivial or satiric contexts. Byron, who mentions Captain Noah and Captain Cook in one breath (*English Bards and Scotch Reviewers*, 356), characterizes Japheth first as a dutiful son, then as a disillusioned rebel who cannot understand why he should be spared when all else perishes ('Heaven and Earth'). In Emily Brontë's *Wuthering Heights*, the self-righteous Joseph, like the

103

drunken Joseph Poorgrass in Hardy's *Far from the Madding Crowd*, invokes the memory of Noah. The patriarch as a discoverer of wine is referred to in Scott's *Anne of Geierstein*, Melville's *The Confidence-Man*, and Twain's *The Mysterious Stranger*. In Kipling's 'Sappers' Noah appears as the builder of the first pontoon, one who would not have become drunk if he had trained with Her Majesty's Royal Engineers. Peepy in Dickens' *Bleak House* replays the drunkenness of Noah by dipping a toy figure of Noah 'head first into the wine-glasses' (chapter 30). Daniel Webster is indirectly compared to Noah in Whittier's antislavery poem 'Ichabod', the last stanza of which alludes to Genesis 9:23.

In the 20th century Noah appears in a variety of guises. Whereas science-fiction writers such as G.P. Serviss (*The Second Deluge*) and A.C. Clarke (*The Songs of Distant Earth*) turn him into a worldly scientist, C. Day Lewis transforms him into a bourgeois willing to join the rebellion of the proletariat (*Noah and the Waters*). In H.G. Wells' *All Aboard for Ararat* he becomes a utopian novelist, in Golding's *The Spire* an ambitious church-builder, and in Burgess' *End of the World News* first the builder of a space ark, then a Nazi-like leader, and finally an imaginative science-fiction writer. In Malamud's *God's Grace*, Cohn, the sole human survivor of an atomic war, compares himself to Noah.

In Connelly's *Green Pastures* Noah is a black preacher. In Odets' *The Flowering Peach* he is a heavy drinker even before the flood, a worried father, and a man who, however unhappy with God's commands, learns humility. He appears as a cruel brother in Robert Coover's story 'The Brother', and as a stern patriarch married to a humane wife in David Garnett's novel *Two by Two*. Timothy Findley, in *Not Wanted on the Voyage*, sees Noah as an experimenter, a disciplinarian, and a pitiable man who, since God remains silent, has to seek refuge in cheap tricks.

The story of how Noah is discovered in his shame is the subject of Zora Neale Hurston's play 'The First One', which stresses Ham's willingness to leave his family and accept his fate as a black man. James Joyce, in *Ulysses*, implicitly compares Bloom to the patriarch by describing Stephen as a Japheth in search of a father.

Paul Goetsch
Freiburg Universität, Freiburg, Germany

Potiphar's Wife

The story of Joseph and Potiphar's wife is found in Genesis 39:7–20. Potiphar, an Egyptian official, bought Joseph from the Midianites, to whom he had been sold by his brothers in a jealous rage (Genesis 37:28, 36). Potiphar made him an overseer of his house and finally left all he had in Joseph's hand (39:6). When Potiphar's wife 'cast her eyes upon' the young slave and tried to seduce him, he fled, leaving his garment in her hand. She then slandered him (claiming that he had tried to rape her), and consequently her husband cast Joseph into prison. This incident is alluded to in Jubilees 39 and in the Testament of Joseph (in The Testaments of the Twelve Patriarchs), where it becomes the basis of an extended exhortation to chastity. These and other extracanonical Jewish sources provide elaborate embellishment of the temptation scene as well as dramatic heightening: Joseph is made to feel, if only fleetingly, a sinful passion for his mistress.

In the 17th century the story is frequently used as an illustration of the virtue of chastity. Bunyan, in *The Life and Death of Mr Badman* (chapter 4), contrasts Joseph's behaviour with that of Mr Badman and his fellows. He goes on to state that many women are made 'whores', like Potiphar's wife, 'by the flatteries of Badman's fellows' and even by promises of marriage. In *Pilgrim's Progress*, Potiphar's wife turns up in the allegorical figure Wanton, who tries to seduce Christian's companion Faithful. He recognizes her hypocrisy in many who 'cry out against sin in the Pulpit,… yet can abide it well enough in the heart, and house, and conversation'. Christiana's son Joseph is exhorted to be like his Old Testament namesake – 'Chast, and one that flies from Temptation'.

Laurence Sterne tells the story of the 'shameless woman' in order to 'recommend chastity as the noblest male qualification' – '…the malice and falsehood of the disappointed woman naturally arose on that occasion, and there is but a short step from the practice of virtue, to the hatred of it' (*Guardian*, no. 45). Potiphar's wife turns up in Henry Fielding's *Joseph Andrews* (1.5), in the character of Lady Booby, who unsuccessfully attempts to seduce her young servant. Having proved himself to be a model of chastity, he is called Joseph, after his biblical namesake, throughout the remainder of the novel.

Joseph's chastity is also alluded to by Surface in Sheridan's *School for Scandal*, when he tries to protect Lady Teazle (hidden behind a screen in his room) from her husband. He pretends that he is a rogue and the hidden person a French girl: '... tho' I hold a man of Intrigue to be a most despicable Character – yet you know it doesn't follow that one is to be an absolute Joseph either' (4.3). Byron refers to the story in a similarly piquant situation of his *Don Juan* (1.186), and other allusions to 'Dame Potiphar' are made in Sir Walter Scott's novel *Woodstock* (chapter 25), and in Anthony Trollope's *The Last Chronicle of Barset* (chapter 51). Keats calls Fame a 'Gipsey' and a 'Sister-in-law to jealous Potiphar', referring to her fickleness ('On Fame').

The garment left behind by Joseph plays both a real and a figurative role in a number of 19th-century works. William Blake repeatedly describes Joseph's many-coloured coat as being stripped off by women, evidently in reminiscence of the incident with Potiphar's wife. Emerson admonishes his readers in his essay 'Self-Reliance' not to rely on their memories but on the present: 'Leave your theory, as Joseph his coat in the hand of the harlot, and flee'. In 'Hippolytus Veiled', Walter Pater echoes the biblical tale when he causes Hippolytus to flee from Phaedra's seductive advances, 'his vesture remaining in her hands'. When the husband returns suddenly, she tells him a false story 'of violence to her bed', and he believes her.

In a passage of good-humoured narrative irony in Herman Melville's *Redburn* (chapter 17) the pious black cook Thompson uses the story to admonish the ship's steward, a 'sad profligate and gay deceiver ashore'. In modern American literature Saul Bellow makes the account of Potiphar's wife the object of a Hebrew lesson in one of Moses Herzog's *heder* reminiscences (*Herzog*, Viking ed., 131).

Manfred Siebald
Johannes Gutenberg Universität, Mainz, Germany

Rachel

Rachel (in Hebrew, 'ewe') was the younger daughter of Laban the Haranite, and the second wife of Jacob, even though she had been betrothed to him first (Genesis 29). She bore two sons: Joseph, who was later to save the twelve tribes of Israel from famine and through whom Rachel was later identified with the Northern Kingdom (Jeremiah 31:15), and Benjamin. Five specific associations with Rachel create literary allusions: (1) she was loved by Jacob, who served fourteen years for her; (2) she was barren while her sister bore children; (3) she bartered with Leah in order to win a night with Jacob; (4) she cleverly stole her father's *teraphim* or household gods; (5) she was identified with Israel as a mother weeping inconsolably for her children who 'were not' (Jeremiah 31:15; Matthew 2:18).

In English literature, Rachel the mourning mother is alluded to with considerable frequency. In Chaucer's *Prioress' Tale* (7.627), the slain boy's mother is a 'newer Rachel' as she swoons by his bier. Melville's *Moby Dick* describes the captain of the *Rachel* hunting for a lost son, weeping for children who are not. Charles Lamb ('In Praise of Chimney Sweepers') describes many noble Rachels weeping for their children, referring to the Victorian practice of abduction of boys for the sweep trade. In T.S. Eliot's *The Waste Land*, a 'murmur of maternal lamentation' (367) recalls Rachel's inconsolable grief.

Associations with the Genesis narrative inform the characterization of Rachael in Dickens' *Hard Times*. Thirty-five, unmarried, and childless, Rachael is loved by Stephen Blackpool, who wants to marry her even though he is already married to a drunkard; he must work (to afford a divorce) in order to marry Rachael. Rachel Ray in Trollope's novel of that name can be won only after service on the part of Luke; Angel Clare in Hardy's *Tess of the D'Urbervilles* has 'three Leahs to get one Rachel' (chapter 23). Thackeray's novel *Henry Esmond* is the story of a man's service for Rachel, whom he loves but who spurns him, his subsequent labours for another woman, and his final marriage to Rachel. (The same theme is treated ironically by Thackeray in the sequel, *The Virginians*.) Rachel's barrenness is considered in the 20th-century novel by Margaret Laurence, *A Jest of God*. An unmarried, 34-year-old younger sister, Rachel has an affair which she believes results in pregnancy but which in fact turns out to be a benign tumour which is surgically removed; bereft of both child and lover, she is left only with a childish old mother and the sense that God has somehow made a joke of her daring to sin.

Linda Beamer
Ryerson Polytechnic Institute, Toronto, Ontario

Rebecca

Daughter of Bethuel of Paddan-aram (Genesis 22:23) and sister of Laban (Genesis 24:29), Rebecca is principally noteworthy as the wife of Isaac (Genesis 24:1–67) and mother of Jacob and Esau (Genesis 25:21–26). Rebecca aided the younger son in obtaining Isaac's paternal blessing by deception (Genesis 27:1–45). She is mentioned by Paul (Romans 9:10), along with Sarah, as one through whom God chose to fulfil the promise to Abraham.

In medieval art Rebecca is usually depicted as the exemplary bride at the well, serving the camels of Isaac's slave, as the crafty servant of God hiding in the background while Jacob obtains the blessing, or as the bride of Christ (Ecclesia) holding her pitcher or adorned with bracelets and earrings.

After the medieval period Rebecca virtually disappears as a reference or subject in English literature. She enjoys an attractive role in Henry Vaughan's 'Isaac's Marriage' (circa 1650), a poem in *Silex Scintillans* based on Genesis 24:63, where Isaac, at eventide, awaits the arrival of his bride – that 'lovely object of thy thought', chaste, with virginal blushes and fears, bearing her pitcher, 'O sweet, divine simplicity'. But no mention of her is made in Spenser, Shakespeare, Milton, or the metaphysical poets of the 17th century. She is given one line in Dryden's 'To my Honour'd Kinsman, John Driden', where Driden, a second son, is likened to 'Rebecca's Heir' (43). She is mentioned in Pope's paraphrase of Chaucer's *Merchant's Tale*, in a list of virtuous women based on Albertano, but credit for the reference there goes to Chaucer.

Matthew Arnold mentions her in 'The Future', where her innocence is contrasted with the evils of industrial society –

> What girl
> Now reads in her bosom as clear
> As Rebecca read, when she sate
> At eve by the palm-shaded well?
> Who guards in her breast
> As deep, as pellucid a spring
> Of feeling, as tranquil, as sure?

But in the 19th century she mainly contributes a name, perhaps with erotic overtones, as in Coleridge's 'Black ey'd Rebecca', the epitome of woman's wiles in 'The Wills of the Wisp', and especially in Scott's *Ivanhoe*, with its beautiful Jewess heroine, burlesqued by Thackeray in *Rebecca and Rowena*.

Russell A. Peck
University of Rochester

Sarah

The first of the four Old Testament matriarchs and the first of Abraham's two wives is introduced in Genesis 11:29–30 as Sarai (Hebrew 'princess'), an archaic form, which God changes to Sarah in Genesis 17:15. Sarah dies in Hebron at age 127 and is buried in what becomes the ancestral burying ground, the cave of Machpelah (Genesis 23:1–20).

In pre-Romantic English literature, Sarah is something of a stock figure. In the Old English *Genesis* (1719–2767) she is the archetypal matriarch; in the Middle English *Genesis and Exodus* and *Metrical Paraphrase of the Old Testament* she is, additionally, the faithful Sarah of Hebrews 11:11 superimposed on the narrative of Genesis 12–21. In *Cleanness* Sarah's obedience, faith, and fruitfulness are contrasted to the disobedience, impiety, and sterility of Lot's wife and of the Sodomites. In Chaucer's *Merchant's Tale* (*Canterbury Tales* 4.1703–1705) Sarah is held up as an example of the perfect wife for youthful May to emulate. One literary remembrance of Sarah's feminine appeal is in Burns' song 'Ken ye ought o' Captain Grose?', which asks, 'Is he to Abram's bosom gane? /... Or haudin Sarah by the wame?' (13, 15).

Dramatic adaptations of Isaac's being sacrificed occasionally feature Sarah as a foil for Abraham. The Dublin Abraham play (*Non-Cyclic Plays and Fragments*, ed. N. Davis, 1970) is the first of these and the only English medieval drama which includes Sarah. Later adaptations tend to follow a fairly consistent plot and theme; typically, Sarah's maternal attachment to Isaac causes her to oppose the journey to Moriah, but when Isaac returns unharmed, she praises God. There are, however, interesting variations. In the Dublin Abraham play,

Abraham's fears that Sarah will not understand the purpose of his journey are a projection of his own doubts onto her. In Arthur Golding's translation of Theodore Beza's *Tragedie of Abraham's Sacrifice* (1577), a lively argument between Sarah and Abraham (386–421) develops the contrast between the 'natural man' and the man of faith. In George Lesley's 'Abraham's Faith' (*Divine Dialogues*, 1678), Sarah is uncharacteristically trusting, despite her dream of a heavenly bow which shoots Isaac; she nevertheless displays extravagant jealousy of Hagar. In *The Trial of Abraham* (1790) by a Mr Farrer, Sarah's objections to Abraham's journey are so exaggerated that she outdoes Shakespeare's weeping queens. A recent play in this vein is Laurence Housman's *Abraham and Isaac*, which strips away the miraculous so that the characters must discover God within themselves; Housman's chief departure from his predecessors, however, is to deny Sarah the understanding of God which Abraham and Isaac ultimately achieve.

Apart from poetry and drama based specifically on Genesis, Sarah makes few appearances in English literature. J. Vogel, however, has observed that the many prominent Sarahs in Dickens, all 'jealous, crabbed, reactionary, wizened, primitive-souled' (*Allegory in Dickens*, 1977, 278), are based on the Old Testament Sarah. One of the more remarkable Sarahs in recent literature is in Archibald MacLeish's drama *J.B.* (1956), an adaptation of the Job story set in modern America. MacLeish's Sarah is the wife of the successful, life-loving businessman J.B., with whom she shares the loss of her children – Rebecca, Ruth, David, Jonathan, and Mary. Although J.B. is Job-like throughout, Sarah falls from piety into despair before her faith is resurrected in the likeness of her husband's.

M.W. Twomey
Ithaca College

GENESIS

Part One: The Beginning of the World

Part Two: The God of Abraham

Part Three: Jacob and Esau

Part Four: Joseph and his Brothers

The Beginning of the World

THE CREATION
Genesis 1:1 – 2:3

In the beginning God created the heavens and the earth. The earth was a vast waste, darkness covered the deep, and the spirit of God hovered over the surface of the water. God said, 'Let there be light,' and there was light; and God saw the light was good, and he separated light from darkness. He called the light day, and the darkness night. So evening came, and morning came; it was the first day.

God said, 'Let there be a vault between the waters, to separate water from water.' So God made the vault, and separated the water under the vault from the water above it, and so it was; and God called the vault the heavens. Evening came, and morning came, the second day.

God said, 'Let the water under the heavens be gathered into one place, so that dry land may appear'; and so it was. God called the dry land earth, and the gathering of the water he called sea; and God saw that it was good.

Then God said, 'Let the earth produce growing things; let there be on the earth plants that bear seed, and trees bearing fruit each with its own kind of seed.' So it was; the earth produced growing things: plants bearing their own kind of seed and trees bearing fruit, each with its own kind of seed; and God saw that it was good. Evening came, and morning came, the third day.

God said, 'Let there be lights in the vault of the heavens to separate day from night, and let them serve as signs both for festivals and for seasons and years. Let them also shine in the heavens to give light on earth.' So it was; God made two great lights, the greater to govern the day and the lesser to govern the night; he also made the stars. God put these lights in the vault of the heavens to give light on earth, to govern day and night, and to separate light from darkness; and God saw that it was good. Evening came, and morning came, the fourth day.

God said, 'Let the water teem with living creatures, and let birds fly above the earth across the vault of the heavens.' God then created the great sea-beasts and all living creatures that move and swarm in the water, according to their various kinds, and every kind of bird; and God saw that it was good. He blessed them and said, 'Be fruitful and increase; fill the water of the sea, and let the birds increase on the land.' Evening came, and morning came, the fifth day.

God said, 'Let the earth bring forth living creatures, according to their various kinds: cattle, creeping things, and wild animals, all according to their various kinds.' So it was; God made wild animals, cattle, and every creeping thing, all according to their various kinds; and he saw that it was good. Then God said, 'Let us make human beings in our image, after our likeness, to have dominion over the fish in the sea, the birds of the air, the cattle, all wild animals on land, and everything that creeps on the earth.'

God created human beings in his own image;
in the image of God he created them;
male and female he created them.

God blessed them and said to them, 'Be fruitful and increase, fill the earth and subdue it, have dominion over the fish in the sea, the birds of the air, and every living thing that moves on the earth.'

God also said, 'Throughout the earth I give you all plants that bear seed, and every tree that bears fruit with seed: they shall be yours for food. All green plants I give for food to the wild animals, to all the birds of the air, and to everything that creeps on the earth, every living creature.' So it was; and God saw all that he had made, and it was very good. Evening came, and morning came, the sixth day.

Thus the heavens and the earth and everything in them were completed. On the sixth day God brought to an end all the work he had been doing; on the seventh day, having finished all his work, God blessed the day and made it holy, because it was the day he finished all his work of creation.

THE GARDEN OF EDEN
Genesis 2:4–9, 15–25

This is the story of the heavens and the earth after their creation.

When the Lord God made the earth and the heavens, there was neither shrub nor plant growing on the earth, because the Lord God had sent no rain; nor was there anyone to till the ground. Moisture used to well up out of the earth and water all the surface of the ground.

The Lord God formed a human being from the dust of the ground and breathed into his nostrils the breath of life, so that he became a living creature. The Lord God planted a garden in Eden away to the east, and in it he put the man he had formed. The Lord God made trees grow up from the ground, every kind of tree pleasing to the eye and good for food; and in the middle of the garden he set the tree of life and the tree of the knowledge of good and evil...

The Lord God took the man and put him in the garden of Eden to till it and look after it. 'You may eat from any tree in the garden', he told the man, 'except from the tree of the knowledge of good and evil; the day you eat from that, you are surely doomed to die.' Then the Lord God said, 'It is not good for the man to be alone; I shall make a partner suited to him.' So from the earth he formed all the wild animals and all the birds of the air, and brought them to the man to see what he would call them; whatever the man called each living creature, that would be its name. The man gave names to all cattle, to the birds of the air, and to every wild animal; but for the man himself no suitable partner was found. The Lord God then put the man into a deep sleep and, while he slept, he took one of the man's ribs and closed up the flesh over the place. The rib he had taken out of the man the Lord God built up into a woman, and he brought her to the man. The man said:

This one at last
is bone from my bones,
flesh from my flesh!
She shall be called woman,
for from man was she taken.

That is why a man leaves his father and mother and attaches himself to his wife, and the two become one. Both were naked, the man and his wife, but they had no feeling of shame.

THE FALL
Genesis 3

The serpent, which was the most cunning of all the creatures the Lord God had made, asked the woman, 'Is it true that God has forbidden you to eat from any tree in the garden?' She replied, 'We may eat the fruit of any tree in the garden, except for the tree in the middle of the garden. God has forbidden us to eat the fruit of that tree or even to touch it; if we do, we shall die.'

'Of course you will not die,' said the serpent; 'for God knows that, as soon as you eat it, your eyes will be opened and you will be like God himself, knowing both good and evil.'

The woman looked at the tree: the fruit would be good to eat; it was pleasing to the eye and desirable for the knowledge it could give. So she took some and ate it; she also gave some to her husband, and he ate it. Then the eyes of both of them were opened, and they knew that they were naked; so they stitched fig-leaves together and made themselves loincloths.

The man and his wife heard the sound of the Lord God walking about in the garden at the time of the evening breeze, and they hid from him among the trees. The Lord God called to the man, 'Where are you?' He replied, 'I heard the sound of you in the garden and I was afraid because I was naked, so I hid.' God said, 'Who told you that you were naked? Have you eaten from the tree which I forbade you to eat from?'

The man replied, 'It was the woman you gave to be with me who gave me fruit from the tree, and I ate it.' The Lord God said to the woman, 'What have you done?' The woman answered, 'It was the serpent who deceived me into eating it.' Then the Lord God said to the serpent:

'Because you have done this you are cursed alone of all cattle and the creatures of the wild.

On your belly you will crawl,
and dust you will eat
all the days of your life.
I shall put enmity between you and the woman,
between your brood and hers.
They will strike at your head,
and you will strike at their heel.

To the woman he said:

I shall give you great labour in childbearing;
with labour you will bear children.
You will desire your husband,
but he will be your master.

And to the man he said: 'Because you have listened to your wife and
have eaten from the tree which I forbade you,

on your account the earth will be cursed.
You will get your food from it only by labour
all the days of your life;
it will yield thorns and thistles for you.
You will eat of the produce of the field,
and only by the sweat of your brow will you
    win your bread
until you return to the earth;
for from it you were taken.
Dust you are, to dust you will return.'

The man named his wife Eve because she was the mother of all living
beings. The Lord God made coverings from skins for the man and his
wife and clothed them. But he said, 'The man has become like one of
us, knowing good and evil; what if he now reaches out and takes fruit
from the tree of life also, and eats it and lives for ever?'

So the Lord God banished him from the garden of Eden to till
the ground from which he had been taken. When he drove him out,
God settled him to the east of the garden of Eden, and he stationed
the cherubim and a sword whirling and flashing to guard the way to
the tree of life.

CAIN AND ABEL
Genesis 4:1–16, 25, 26

The man lay with his wife Eve, and she conceived and gave birth to Cain. She said, 'With the help of the Lord I have brought into being a male child.' Afterwards she had another child, Abel. He tended the flock, and Cain worked the land. In due season Cain brought some of the fruits of the earth as an offering to the Lord, while Abel brought the choicest of the firstborn of his flock. The Lord regarded Abel and his offering with favour, but not Cain and his offering. Cain was furious and he glowered. The Lord said to Cain,

> Why are you angry? Why are you scowling?
> If you do well, you hold your head up;
> if not, sin is a demon crouching at the door;
> it will desire you, and you will be mastered by it.

Cain said to his brother Abel, 'Let us go out into the country.' Once there, Cain attacked and murdered his brother. The Lord asked Cain, 'Where is your brother Abel?' 'I do not know,' Cain answered. 'Am I my brother's keeper?' The Lord said, 'What have you done? Your brother's blood is crying out to me from the ground. Now you are accursed and will be banished from the very ground which has opened its mouth to receive the blood you have shed. When you till the ground, it will no longer yield you its produce. You shall be a wanderer, a fugitive on the earth.' Cain said to the Lord, 'My punishment is heavier than I can bear; now you are driving me off the land, and I must hide myself from your presence. I shall be a wanderer, a fugitive on the earth, and I can be killed at sight by anyone.' The Lord answered him, 'No: if anyone kills Cain, sevenfold vengeance will be exacted from him.' The Lord put a mark on Cain, so that anyone happening to meet him should not kill him. Cain went out from the Lord's presence and settled in the land of Nod to the east of Eden...

Adam lay with his wife again. She gave birth to a son, and named him Seth, 'for', she said, 'God has granted me another son in place of Abel, because Cain killed him'. Seth too had a son, whom he named Enosh. At that time people began to invoke the Lord by name.

NOAH AND THE FLOOD
Genesis 6; 7:11–19, 22–24; 8:1–19; 9:8–29

The human race began to increase and to spread over the earth and daughters were born to them. The sons of the gods saw how beautiful these daughters were, so they took for themselves such women as they chose. But the Lord said, 'My spirit will not remain in a human being for ever; because he is mortal flesh, he will live only for a hundred and twenty years.'

In those days as well as later, when the sons of the gods had intercourse with the daughters of mortals and children were born to them, the Nephilim were on the earth; they were the heroes of old, people of renown.

When the Lord saw how great was the wickedness of human beings on earth, and how their every thought and inclination were always wicked, he bitterly regretted that he had made mankind on earth. He said, 'I shall wipe off the face of the earth this human race which I have created – yes, man and beast, creeping things and birds. I regret that I ever made them.' Noah, however, had won the Lord's favour.

This is the story of Noah. Noah was a righteous man, the one blameless man of his time, and he walked with God. He had three sons: Shem, Ham, and Japheth. God saw that the world was corrupt and full of violence; and seeing this corruption, for the life of everyone on earth was corrupt, God said to Noah, 'I am going to bring the whole human race to an end, for because of them the earth is full of violence. I am about to destroy them, and the earth along with them. Make yourself an ark with ribs of cypress; cover it with reeds and coat it inside and out with pitch. This is to be its design: the length of the ark is to be three hundred cubits, its breadth fifty cubits, and its height thirty cubits. You are to make a roof for the ark, giving it a fall of one cubit when complete; put a door in the side of the ark, and build three decks, lower, middle, and upper. I am about to bring the waters of the flood over the earth to destroy from under heaven every human being that has the spirit of life; everything on earth shall perish. But with you I shall make my covenant, and you will go into the ark, you with your sons, your wife, and your sons' wives. You are

119

to bring living creatures of every kind into the ark to keep them alive with you, two of each kind, a male and a female; two of every kind of bird, beast, and creeping thing are to come to you to be kept alive. See that you take and store by you every kind of food that can be eaten; this will be food for you and for them.' Noah carried out exactly all God had commanded him...

In the year when Noah was six hundred years old, on the seventeenth day of the second month, that very day all the springs of the great deep burst out, the windows of the heavens were opened, and rain fell on the earth for forty days and forty nights. That was the day Noah went into the ark with his sons, Shem, Ham, and Japheth, his own wife, and his three sons' wives. Wild animals of every kind, cattle of every kind, every kind of thing that creeps on the ground, and winged birds of every kind – all living creatures came two by two to Noah in the ark. Those which came were one male and one female of all living things; they came in as God had commanded Noah, and the Lord closed the door on him.

The flood continued on the earth for forty days, and the swelling waters lifted up the ark so that it rose high above the ground. The ark floated on the surface of the swollen waters as they increased over the earth. They increased more and more until they covered all the high mountains everywhere under heaven... Everything on dry land died, everything that had the breath of life in its nostrils. God wiped out every living creature that existed on earth, man and beast, creeping thing and bird; they were all wiped out over the whole earth, and only Noah and those who were with him in the ark survived.

When the water had increased over the earth for a hundred and fifty days, God took thought for Noah and all the beasts and cattle with him in the ark, and he caused a wind to blow over the earth, so that the water began to subside. The springs of the deep and the windows of the heavens were stopped up, the downpour from the skies was checked. Gradually the water receded from the earth, and by the end of a hundred and fifty days it had abated. On the seventeenth day of the seventh month the ark grounded on the mountains of Ararat. The water continued to abate until the tenth month, and on the first day of the tenth month the tops of the mountains could be seen.

At the end of forty days Noah opened the hatch that he had made in the ark, and sent out a raven; it continued flying to and fro until the water on the earth had dried up. Then Noah sent out a dove to see whether the water on the earth had subsided. But the dove found no place where she could settle because all the earth was under water, and so she came back to him in the ark. Noah reached out and caught her, and brought her into the ark. He waited seven days more and again sent out the dove from the ark. She came back to him towards evening with a freshly plucked olive leaf in her beak. Noah knew then that the water had subsided from the earth's surface. He waited yet another seven days and, when he sent out the dove, she did not come back to him. So it came about that, on the first day of the first month of his six hundred and first year, the water had dried up on the earth, and when Noah removed the hatch and looked out, he saw that the ground was dry.

By the twenty-seventh day of the second month the earth was dry, and God spoke to Noah. 'Come out of the ark together with your wife, your sons, and their wives,' he said. 'Bring out every living creature that is with you, live things of every kind, birds, beasts, and creeping things, and let them spread over the earth and be fruitful and increase on it.' So Noah came out with his sons, his wife, and his sons' wives, and all the animals, creeping things, and birds; everything that moves on the ground came out of the ark, one kind after another...

God said to Noah and his sons: 'I am now establishing my covenant with you and with your descendants after you, and with every living creature that is with you, all birds and cattle, all the animals with you on earth, all that have come out of the ark. I shall sustain my covenant with you: never again will all living creatures be destroyed by the waters of a flood, never again will there be a flood to lay waste the earth.'

God said, 'For all generations to come, this is the sign which I am giving of the covenant between myself and you and all living creatures with you:

My bow I set in the clouds
to be a sign of the covenant

between myself and the earth.
When I bring clouds over the earth,
the rainbow will appear in the clouds.

'Then I shall remember the covenant which I have made with you and with all living creatures, and never again will the waters become a flood to destroy all creation. Whenever the bow appears in the cloud, I shall see it and remember the everlasting covenant between God and living creatures of every kind on earth.' So God said to Noah, 'This is the sign of the covenant which I have established with all that lives on earth.'

The sons of Noah who came out of the ark were Shem, Ham, and Japheth; Ham was the father of Canaan. These three were the sons of Noah, and their descendants spread over the whole earth.

Noah, who was the first tiller of the soil, planted a vineyard. He drank so much of the wine that he became drunk and lay naked inside his tent. Ham, father of Canaan, saw his father naked, and went out and told his two brothers. Shem and Japheth took a cloak, put it on their shoulders, and, walking backwards, covered their father's naked body. They kept their faces averted, so that they did not see his nakedness. When Noah woke from his drunkenness and learnt what his youngest son had done to him, he said:

> Cursed be Canaan!
> Most servile of slaves
> shall he be to his brothers.

And he went on:

> Bless, O Lord,
> the tents of Shem;
> may Canaan be his slave.
> May God extend Japheth's boundaries,
> let him dwell in the tents of Shem,
> may Canaan be his slave.

After the flood Noah lived for three hundred and fifty years; he was nine hundred and fifty years old when he died.

THE TOWER OF BABEL
Genesis 11:1–9

There was a time when all the world spoke a single language and used the same words. As people journeyed in the east, they came upon a plain in the land of Shinar and settled there. They said to one another, 'Come, let us make bricks and bake them hard'; they used bricks for stone and bitumen for mortar. Then they said, 'Let us build ourselves a city and a tower with its top in the heavens and make a name for ourselves, or we shall be dispersed over the face of the earth.' The Lord came down to see the city and tower which they had built, and he said, 'Here they are, one people with a single language, and now they have started to do this; from now on nothing they have a mind to do will be beyond their reach. Come, let us go down there and confuse their language, so that they will not understand what they say to one another.' So the Lord dispersed them from there all over the earth, and they left off building the city. That is why it is called Babel, because there the Lord made a babble of the language of the whole world. It was from that place the Lord scattered people over the face of the earth.

Part Two

The God of Abraham

THE PROMISED LAND
Genesis 11:27 – 12:9

These are the descendants of Terah. Terah was the father of Abram, Nahor, and Haran. Haran was Lot's father. Haran died in the land of his birth, Ur of the Chaldees, during his father's lifetime. Abram and Nahor married wives; Abram's wife was called Sarai, and Nahor's Milcah. She was the daughter of Haran, father of Milcah and Iscah. Sarai was barren; she had no child. Terah took his son Abram, his grandson Lot the son of Haran, and his daughter-in-law Sarai, Abram's wife, and they set out from Ur of the Chaldees for Canaan. But when they reached Harran, they settled there. Terah was two hundred and five years old when he died in Harran.

The Lord said to Abram, 'Leave your own country, your kin, and your father's house, and go to a country that I will show you. I shall make you into a great nation; I shall bless you and make your name so great that it will be used in blessings:

those who bless you, I shall bless;
those who curse you, I shall curse.
All the peoples on earth
will wish to be blessed as you are blessed.'

Abram, who was seventy-five years old when he left Harran, set out as the Lord had bidden him, and Lot went with him. He took his wife Sarai, his brother's son Lot, and all the possessions they had gathered and the dependants they had acquired in Harran, and they departed for Canaan. When they arrived there, Abram went on as far as the sanctuary at Shechem, the terebinth tree of Moreh. (At that time the Canaanites lived in the land.) When the Lord appeared to him and

125

said, 'I am giving this land to your descendants,' Abram built an altar there to the Lord who had appeared to him. From there he moved on to the hill-country east of Bethel and pitched his tent between Bethel on the west and Ai on the east. He built there an altar to the Lord whom he invoked by name. Thus Abram journeyed by stages towards the Negeb.

STRANGERS IN EGYPT
Genesis 12:10 – 13:4

The land was stricken by a famine so severe that Abram went down to Egypt to live there for a time. As he was about to enter Egypt, he said to his wife Sarai, 'I am well aware that you are a beautiful woman, and I know that when the Egyptians see you and think, "She is his wife," they will let you live but they will kill me. Tell them you are my sister, so that all may go well with me because of you, and my life be spared on your account.'

When Abram arrived in Egypt, the Egyptians saw that Sarai was indeed very beautiful, and Pharaoh's courtiers, when they saw her, sang her praises to Pharaoh. She was taken into Pharaoh's household, and he treated Abram well because of her, and Abram acquired sheep and cattle and donkeys, male and female slaves, she-donkeys, and camels.

But when the Lord inflicted plagues on Pharaoh and his household on account of Abram's wife Sarai, Pharaoh summoned Abram. 'Why have you treated me like this?' he said. 'Why did you not tell me she was your wife? Why did you say she was your sister, so that I took her as a wife? Here she is: take her and go.' Pharaoh gave his men orders, and they sent Abram on his way with his wife and all that belonged to him.

From Egypt Abram went up into the Negeb, he and his wife and all that he possessed, and Lot went with him. Abram had become very rich in cattle and in silver and gold. From the Negeb he journeyed by stages towards Bethel, to the place between Bethel and Ai where he had earlier pitched his tent, and where he had previously set up an altar and invoked the Lord by name.

ABRAM AND LOT
Genesis 13:5 – 14:1–3, 10–24

Since Lot, who was travelling with Abram, also possessed sheep and cattle and tents, the land could not support them while they were together. They had so much livestock that they could not settle in the same district, and quarrels arose between Abram's herdsmen and Lot's. (The Canaanites and the Perizzites were then living in the land.) Abram said to Lot, 'There must be no quarrelling between us, or between my herdsmen and yours; for we are close kinsmen. The whole country is there in front of you. Let us part company: if you go north, I shall go south; if you go south, I shall go north.' Lot looked around and saw how well watered the whole plain of Jordan was; all the way to Zoar it was like the Garden of the Lord, like the land of Egypt. This was before the Lord had destroyed Sodom and Gomorrah. So Lot chose all the Jordan plain and took the road to the east. They parted company: Abram settled in Canaan, while Lot settled among the cities of the plain and pitched his tent near Sodom. Now the men of Sodom in their wickedness had committed monstrous sins against the Lord.

After Lot and Abram had parted, the Lord said to Abram, 'Look around from where you are towards north, south, east, and west: all the land you see I shall give to you and to your descendants for ever. I shall make your descendants countless as the dust of the earth; only if the specks of dust on the ground could be counted could your descendants be counted. Now go through the length and breadth of the land, for I am giving it to you.' Abram moved his tent and settled by the terebinths of Mamre at Hebron, where he built an altar to the Lord.

In those days King Amraphel of Shinar, King Arioch of Ellasar, King Kedorlaomer of Elam, and King Tidal of Goyim went to war against King Bera of Sodom, King Birsha of Gomorrah, King Shinab of Admah, King Shemeber of Zeboyim, and the king of Bela, which is Zoar. These kings joined forces in the valley of Siddim, which is now the Dead Sea... Now the valley of Siddim was full of bitumen pits, and when the kings of Sodom and Gomorrah fled, some of their men fell into them, but the rest made their escape to the hills. The four kings captured all the flocks and herds of Sodom and Gomorrah and

127

all their provisions, and withdrew, carrying off Abram's nephew, Lot, who was living in Sodom, and his flocks and herds.

A fugitive brought the news to Abram the Hebrew, who at that time had his camp by the terebinths of Mamre the Amorite. This Mamre was the brother of Eshcol and Aner, allies of Abram. When Abram heard that his kinsman had been taken prisoner, he mustered his three hundred and eighteen retainers, men born in his household, and went in pursuit as far as Dan. Abram and his followers surrounded the enemy by night, routed them, and pursued them as far as Hobah, north of Damascus. He recovered all the flocks and herds and also his kinsman Lot with his flocks and herds, together with the women and all his company. On Abram's return from defeating Kedorlaomer and the allied kings, the king of Sodom came out to meet him in the valley of Shaveh, which is now the King's Valley.

Then the king of Salem, Melchizedek, brought food and wine. He was priest of God Most High, and he pronounced this blessing on Abram:

> Blessed be Abram by God Most High,
> Creator of the heavens and the earth.
> And blessed be God Most High,
> who has delivered your enemies into your hand.

Then Abram gave him a tithe of all the booty.

The king of Sodom said to Abram, 'Give me the people, and you can take the livestock.' But Abram replied, 'I lift my hand and swear by the Lord, God Most High, Creator of the heavens and the earth: not a thread or a sandal-thong shall I accept of anything that is yours. You will never say, "I made Abram rich." I shall accept nothing but what the young men have eaten and the share of the men who went with me, Aner, Eshcol, and Mamre; they must have their share.'

A VISION
Genesis 15:1–16

After this the word of the Lord came to Abram in a vision. He said, 'Do not be afraid, Abram; I am your shield. Your reward will be very great.' Abram replied, 'Lord God, what can you give me, seeing that I am childless? The heir to my household is Eliezer of Damascus. You have given me no children, and so my heir must be a slave born in my house.' The word of the Lord came to him: 'This man will not be your heir; your heir will be a child of your own body.' He brought Abram outside and said, 'Look up at the sky, and count the stars, if you can. So many will your descendants be.'

Abram put his faith in the Lord, who reckoned it to him as righteousness, and said, 'I am the Lord who brought you out from Ur of the Chaldees to give you this land as your possession.' Abram asked, 'Lord God, how can I be sure that I shall occupy it?' The Lord answered, 'Bring me a heifer three years old, a she-goat three years old, a ram three years old, a turtle-dove, and a young pigeon.' Abram brought him all these, cut the animals in two, and set the pieces opposite each other, but he did not cut the birds in half. Birds of prey swooped down on the carcasses, but he scared them away. As the sun was going down, Abram fell into a trance and great and fearful darkness came over him. The Lord said to Abram, 'Know this for certain: your descendants will be aliens living in a land that is not their own; they will be enslaved and held in oppression for four hundred years. But I shall punish the nation whose slaves they are, and afterwards they will depart with great possessions. You yourself will join your forefathers in peace and be buried at a ripe old age. But it will be the fourth generation who will return here, for till then the Amorites will not be ripe for punishment.'

HAGAR THE EGYPTIAN
Genesis 16:1 – 17:10, 15–23

Abram's wife Sarai had borne him no children. She had, however, an Egyptian slave-girl named Hagar, and Sarai said to Abram, 'The Lord has not let me have a child. Take my slave-girl; perhaps through her I shall have a son.' Abram heeded what his wife said; so Sarai brought her slave-girl, Hagar the Egyptian, to her husband and gave her to Abram as a wife. When this happened Abram had been in Canaan for ten years. He lay with Hagar and she conceived; and when she knew that she was pregnant, she looked down on her mistress. Sarai complained to Abram, 'I am being wronged; you must do something about it. It was I who gave my slave-girl into your arms, but since she has known that she is pregnant, she has despised me. May the Lord see justice done between you and me.' Abram replied, 'Your slave-girl is in your hands; deal with her as you please.' So Sarai ill-treated her and she ran away from her mistress.

The angel of the Lord came upon Hagar by a spring in the wilderness, the spring on the road to Shur, and he said, 'Hagar, Sarai's slave-girl, where have you come from and where are you going?' She answered, 'I am running away from Sarai my mistress.' The angel of the Lord said to her, 'Go back to your mistress and submit to ill-treatment at her hands.' He also said, 'I shall make your descendants too many to be counted.' The angel of the Lord went on:

> You are with child and will bear a son.
> You are to name him Ishmael,
> because the Lord has heard of your ill-treatment.
> He will be like the wild ass;
> his hand will be against everyone
> and everyone's hand against him;
> and he will live at odds with all his kin.

Hagar called the Lord who spoke to her by the name El-roi, for she said, 'Have I indeed seen God and still live after that vision?' That is why the well is called Beer-lahai-roi; it lies between Kadesh and Bered. Hagar bore Abram a son, and he named the child she bore him Ishmael. Abram was eighty-six years old when she bore Ishmael.

When Abram was ninety-nine years old, the Lord appeared to him and said, 'I am God Almighty. Live always in my presence and be blameless, so that I may make my covenant with you and give you many descendants.' Abram bowed low, and God went on, 'This is my covenant with you: you are to be the father of many nations. Your name will no longer be Abram, but Abraham; for I shall make you father of many nations. I shall make you exceedingly fruitful; I shall make nations out of you, and kings shall spring from you. I shall maintain my covenant with you and your descendants after you, generation after generation, an everlasting covenant: I shall be your

God, yours and your descendants'. As a possession for all time I shall give you and your descendants after you the land in which you now are aliens, the whole of Canaan, and I shall be their God.'

God said to Abraham, 'For your part, you must keep my covenant, you and your descendants after you, generation by generation. This is how you are to keep this covenant between myself and you and your descendants after you: circumcise yourselves, every male among you...

God said to Abraham, 'As for Sarai your wife, you are to call her not Sarai, but Sarah. I shall bless her and give you a son by her. I shall bless her and she will be the mother of nations; from her kings of peoples will spring.' Abraham bowed low, and laughing said to himself, 'Can a son be born to a man who is a hundred years old? Can Sarah bear a child at ninety?' He said to God, 'If only Ishmael might enjoy your special favour!' But God replied, 'No; your wife Sarah will bear you a son, and you are to call him Isaac. With him I shall maintain my covenant as an everlasting covenant for his descendants after him. But I have heard your request about Ishmael; I have blessed him and I shall make him fruitful. I shall give him many descendants; he will be father of twelve princes, and I shall raise a great nation from him. But my covenant I shall fulfil with Isaac, whom Sarah will bear to you at this time next year.' When he had finished talking with Abraham, God left him.

Then Abraham took Ishmael his son, everyone who had been born in his household and everyone he had bought, every male in his household, and that same day he circumcised the flesh of their foreskins as God had commanded him.

THE VISIT OF THE ANGELS
Genesis 18

The Lord appeared to Abraham by the terebinths of Mamre, as he was sitting at the opening of his tent in the heat of the day. He looked up and saw three men standing over against him. On seeing them, he hurried from his tent door to meet them. Bowing low he said, 'Sirs, if I have deserved your favour, do not go past your servant without a visit. Let me send for some water so that you may bathe your feet; and rest under this tree, while I fetch a little food so that you may refresh yourselves. Afterwards you may continue the journey which has brought you my way.' They said, 'Very well, do as you say.' So Abraham hurried into the tent to Sarah and said, 'Quick, take three measures of flour, knead it, and make cakes.' He then hastened to the herd, chose a fine, tender calf, and gave it to a servant, who prepared it at once. He took curds and milk and the calf which was now ready, set it all before them, and there under the tree waited on them himself while they ate.

They asked him where Sarah his wife was, and he replied, 'She is in the tent.' One of them said, 'About this time next year I shall come back to you, and your wife Sarah will have a son.' Now Sarah was listening at the opening of the tent close by him. Both Abraham and Sarah were very old, Sarah being well past the age of childbearing. So she laughed to herself and said, 'At my time of life I am past bearing children, and my husband is old.' The Lord said to Abraham, 'Why did Sarah laugh and say, "Can I really bear a child now that I am so old?" Is anything impossible for the Lord? In due season, at this time next year, I shall come back to you, and Sarah will have a son.' Because she was frightened, Sarah lied and denied that she had laughed; but he said, 'Yes, you did laugh.'

The men set out and looked down towards Sodom, and Abraham went with them to see them on their way. The Lord had thought to himself, 'Shall I conceal from Abraham what I am about to do? He will become a great and powerful nation, and all nations on earth will wish to be blessed as he is blessed. I have singled him out so that he may charge his sons and family after him to conform to the way of the Lord and do what is right and just; thus I shall fulfil for him all that I have promised.' The Lord said, 'How great is the outcry over Sodom and Gomorrah! How grave their sin must be! I shall go down and see whether their deeds warrant the outcry reaching me. I must know the truth.' When the men turned and went off towards Sodom, Abraham remained standing before the Lord. Abraham drew near him and asked, 'Will you really sweep away innocent and wicked together? Suppose there are fifty innocent in the city; will you really sweep it away, and not pardon the place because of the fifty innocent there? Far be it from you to do such a thing – to kill innocent and wicked together; for then the innocent would suffer with the wicked. Far be it from you! Should not the judge of all the earth do what is just?' The Lord replied, 'If I find in Sodom fifty innocent, I shall pardon the whole place for their sake.' Abraham said, 'May I make so bold as to speak to the Lord, I who am nothing but dust and ashes: suppose there are five short of fifty innocent? Will you destroy the whole city for the lack of five men?' 'If I find forty-five there,' he replied, 'I shall not destroy it.' Abraham spoke again, 'Suppose forty can be found there?' 'For the sake of the forty I shall not do it,' he replied. Then Abraham said, 'Let not my Lord become angry if I speak again: suppose thirty can be found there?' He answered, 'If I find thirty there, I shall not do it.' Abraham continued, 'May I make so bold as to speak to the Lord: suppose twenty can be found there?' He replied, 'For the sake of the twenty I shall not destroy it.' Abraham said, 'Let not my Lord become angry if I speak just once more: suppose ten can be found there?' 'For the sake of the ten I shall not destroy it,' said the Lord. When the Lord had finished talking to Abraham, he went away, and Abraham returned home.

THE DESTRUCTION OF SODOM
Genesis 19

The two angels came to Sodom in the evening while Lot was sitting by the city gate. When he saw them, he rose to meet them and bowing low he said, 'I pray you, sirs, turn aside to your servant's house to spend the night there and bathe your feet. You can continue your journey in the morning.' 'No,' they answered, 'we shall spend the night in the street.' But Lot was so insistent that they accompanied him into his house. He prepared a meal for them, baking unleavened bread for them to eat.

Before they had lain down to sleep, the men of Sodom, both young and old, everyone without exception, surrounded the house. They called to Lot: 'Where are the men who came to you tonight? Bring them out to us so that we may have intercourse with them.' Lot went out into the doorway to them, and, closing the door behind him, said, 'No, my friends, do not do anything so wicked. Look, I have two daughters, virgins both of them; let me bring them out to you, and you can do what you like with them. But do nothing to these men, because they have come under the shelter of my roof.' They said, 'Out of our way! This fellow has come and settled here as an alien, and does he now take it upon himself to judge us? We will treat you worse than them.' They crowded in on Lot and pressed close to break down the door. But the two men inside reached out, pulled Lot into the house, and shut the door. Then they struck those in the doorway, both young and old, with blindness so that they could not find the entrance.

The two men said to Lot, 'Have you anyone here, sons-in-law, sons, or daughters, or anyone else belonging to you in the city? Get them out of this place, because we are going to destroy it. The Lord is aware of the great outcry against its citizens and has sent us to destroy it.' So Lot went out and urged his sons-in-law to get out of the place at once. 'The Lord is about to destroy the city,' he said. But they did not take him seriously.

As soon as it was dawn, the angels urged Lot: 'Quick, take your wife and your two daughters who are here, or you will be destroyed when the city is punished.' When he delayed, they grabbed his hand and the hands of his wife and two daughters, because the Lord had spared him, and they led him to safety outside the city. After they had brought them out, one said, 'Flee for your lives! Do not look back or stop anywhere in the plain. Flee to the hills or you will be destroyed.' Lot replied, 'No, sirs! You have shown your servant favour, and even more by your unfailing care you have saved my life, but I cannot escape to the hills; I shall be overtaken by the disaster, and die. Look, here is a town, only a small place, near enough for me to get to quickly. Let me escape to this small place and save my life.' He said to him, 'I grant your request: I shall not overthrow the town you speak of. But flee there quickly, because I can do nothing until you are there.' That is why the place was called Zoar. The sun had risen over the land as Lot entered Zoar, and the Lord rained down fire and brimstone from the skies on Sodom and Gomorrah. He overthrew those cities and destroyed all the plain, with everyone living there and everything growing in the ground. But Lot's wife looked back, and she turned into a pillar of salt.

Early next morning Abraham went to the place where he had stood in the presence of the Lord. As he looked over Sodom and Gomorrah and all the wide extent of the plain, he saw thick smoke rising from the earth like smoke from a kiln. Thus it was, when God destroyed the cities of the plain, he took thought for Abraham by rescuing Lot from the total destruction of the cities where he had been living.

Because Lot was afraid to stay in Zoar, he went up from there and settled with his two daughters in the hill-country, where he lived with them in a cave. The elder daughter said to the younger, 'Our father is old and there is not a man in the country to come to us in the usual way. Come now, let us ply our father with wine and then lie with him and in this way preserve the family through our father.' That night they gave him wine to drink, and the elder daughter came and lay with him, and he did not know when she lay down and when she got up. Next day the elder said to the younger, 'Last night I lay with my father. Let us ply him with wine again tonight; then you go in and lie with him. So we shall preserve the family through our father.' They gave their father wine to drink that night also; and the younger daughter went and lay with him, and he did not know when she lay down and when she got up.

In this way both of Lot's daughters came to be pregnant by their father. The elder daughter bore a son and called him Moab; he was the ancestor of the present-day Moabites. The younger also bore a son, whom she called Ben-ammi; he was the ancestor of the present-day Ammonites.

HAGAR AND ISHMAEL
Genesis 21:1–21

The Lord showed favour to Sarah as he had promised, and made good what he had said about her. She conceived and at the time foretold by God she bore a son to Abraham in his old age. The son whom Sarah bore to him Abraham named Isaac, and when Isaac was eight days old Abraham circumcised him, as decreed by God. Abraham was a hundred years old when his son Isaac was born. Sarah said, 'God has given me good reason to laugh, and everyone who hears will laugh with me.' She added, 'Whoever would have told Abraham that Sarah would suckle children? Yet I have borne him a son in his old age.' The boy grew and was weaned, and on the day of his weaning Abraham gave a great feast.

Sarah saw the son whom Hagar the Egyptian had borne to Abraham playing with Isaac, and she said to Abraham, 'Drive out this slave-girl and her son! I will not have this slave's son sharing the inheritance with my son Isaac.' Abraham was very upset at this because of Ishmael, but God said to him, 'Do not be upset for the boy and your slave-girl. Do as Sarah says, because it is through Isaac's line that your name will be perpetuated. I shall make a nation of the slave-girl's son, because he also is your child.'

Early next morning Abraham took some food and a full water-skin and gave them to Hagar. He set the child on her shoulder and sent her away, and she wandered about in the wilderness of Beersheba. When the water in the skin was finished, she thrust the child under a bush, then went and sat down some way off, about a bowshot distant. 'How can I watch the child die?' she said, and sat there, weeping bitterly. God heard the child crying, and the angel of God called from heaven to Hagar, 'What is the matter, Hagar? Do not be afraid: God has heard the child crying where you laid him. Go, lift the child and hold him in your arms, because I shall make of him a great nation.' Then God opened her eyes and she saw a well full of water; she went to it, filled the water-skin, and gave the child a drink. God was with the child as he grew up. He lived in the wilderness of Paran and became an archer; and his mother got him a wife from Egypt.

THE SACRIFICE OF ISAAC
Genesis 22:1–19

Some time later God put Abraham to the test. 'Abraham!' he called to him, and Abraham replied, 'Here I am!' God said, 'Take your son, your one and only son Isaac whom you love, and go to the land of Moriah. There you shall offer him as a sacrifice on one of the heights which I shall show you.' Early in the morning Abraham saddled his donkey, and took with him two of his men and his son Isaac; and having split firewood for the sacrifice, he set out for the place of which God had spoken. On the third day Abraham looked up and saw the shrine in the distance. He said to his men, 'Stay here with the donkey while I and the boy go on ahead. We shall worship there, and then come back to you.'

Abraham took the wood for the sacrifice and put it on his son Isaac's shoulder, while he himself carried the fire and the knife. As the two of them went on together, Isaac spoke. 'Father!' he said. Abraham answered, 'What is it, my son?' Isaac said, 'Here are the fire and the wood, but where is the sheep for a sacrifice?' Abraham answered, 'God will provide himself with a sheep for a sacrifice, my son.' The two of them went on together until they came to the place of which God had spoken. There Abraham built an altar and arranged the wood. He bound his son Isaac and laid him on the altar on top of the wood. He reached out for the knife to slay his son, but the angel of the Lord called to him from heaven, 'Abraham! Abraham!' He answered, 'Here I am!' The angel said, 'Do not raise your hand against the boy; do not touch him. Now I know that you are a godfearing man. You have not withheld from me your son, your only son.' Abraham looked round, and there in a thicket he saw a ram caught by its horns. He went, seized the ram, and offered it as a sacrifice instead of his son. Abraham named that shrine 'The Lord will provide'; and to this day the saying is: 'In the mountain of the Lord it was provided.'

Then the angel of the Lord called from heaven a second time to Abraham and said, 'This is the word of the Lord: By my own self I swear that because you have done this and have not withheld your son, your only son, I shall bless you abundantly and make your descendants as numerous as the stars in the sky or the grains of sand on the seashore. Your descendants will possess the cities of their enemies. All nations on earth will wish to be blessed as your descendants are blessed, because you have been obedient to me.'

Abraham then went back to his men, and together they returned to Beersheba; and there Abraham remained.

THE DEATH OF SARAH
Genesis 23

Sarah lived to be a hundred and twenty-seven years old, and she died
in Kiriath-arba (which is Hebron) in Canaan. Abraham went in to
mourn over Sarah and to weep for her. When at last he rose and left
the presence of his dead one, he approached the Hittites: 'I am an
alien and a settler among you,' he said. 'Make over to me some
ground among you for a burial-place, that I may bury my dead.' The
Hittites answered, 'Listen to us, sir: you are a mighty prince among
us; bury your dead in the best grave we have. There is not one of us
who would deny you his grave or hinder you from burying your
dead.'

Abraham rose and bowing low to the Hittites, the people of that
region, he said to them, 'If you have a mind to help me about the
burial, then listen to me: speak to Ephron son of Zohar on my behalf,
and ask him to grant me the cave that belongs to him at Machpelah,
at the far end of his land. In your presence let him make it over to me
for the full price, so that I may take possession of it as a burial-place.'
Ephron was sitting with the other Hittites and in the hearing of all
who had assembled at the city gate he gave Abraham this answer: 'No,
sir; hear me: I shall make you a gift of the land and also give you the
cave which is on it. In the presence of my people I give it to you; so
bury your dead.' Abraham bowed low before the people and said to
Ephron in their hearing, 'Do you really mean it? But listen to me – let
me give you the price of the land: take it from me, and I shall bury my
dead there.' Ephron answered, 'Listen, sir: land worth four hundred
shekels of silver, what is that between me and you! You may bury your
dead there.' Abraham closed the bargain with him and weighed out
the amount that Ephron had named in the hearing of the Hittites, four
hundred shekels of the standard recognized by merchants.

So the plot of land belonging to Ephron at Machpelah to the
east of Mamre, the plot, the cave that is on it, with all the trees in the
whole area, became the legal possession of Abraham, in the presence
of all the Hittites who had assembled at the city gate. After this
Abraham buried his wife Sarah in the cave on the plot of land at
Machpelah to the east of Mamre, which is Hebron, in Canaan. Thus,

by purchase from the Hittites, the plot and the cave on it became Abraham's possession as a burial-place.

A WIFE FOR ISAAC
Genesis 24

Abraham was by now a very old man, and the Lord had blessed him in all that he did. Abraham said to the servant who had been longest in his service and was in charge of all he owned, 'Give me your solemn oath: I want you to swear by the Lord, the God of heaven and earth, that you will not take a wife for my son from the women of the Canaanites among whom I am living. You must go to my own country and to my own kindred to find a wife for my son Isaac.' 'What if the woman is unwilling to come with me to this country?' the servant asked. 'Must I take your son back to the land you came from?' Abraham said to him, 'On no account are you to take my son back there. The Lord the God of heaven who took me from my father's house and the land of my birth, the Lord who swore to me that he would give this land to my descendants – he will send his angel before you, and you will take a wife from there for my son. If the woman is unwilling to come with you, then you will be released from your oath to me; only you must not take my son back there.' The servant then put his hand under his master Abraham's thigh and swore that oath.

The servant chose ten camels from his master's herds and, with all kinds of gifts from his master, he went to Aram-naharaim, to the town where Nahor lived. Towards evening, the time when the women go out to draw water, he made the camels kneel down by the well outside the town. 'Lord God of my master Abraham,' he said, 'give me good fortune this day; keep faith with my master Abraham. Here I am by the spring, as the women of the town come out to draw water. I shall say to a girl, "Please lower your jar so that I may drink"; and if she answers, "Drink, and I shall water your camels also," let that be the girl whom you intend for your servant Isaac. In this way I shall know that you have kept faith with my master.'

Before he had finished praying, he saw Rebecca coming out with her water-jar on her shoulder. She was the daughter of Bethuel son of Milcah, the wife of Abraham's brother Nahor. The girl was very beautiful and a virgin guiltless of intercourse with any man. She went down to the spring, filled her jar, and came up again. Abraham's servant hurried to meet her and said, 'Will you give me a little water from your jar?' 'Please drink, sir,' she answered, and at once lowered her jar on to her hand to let him drink. When she had finished giving him a drink, she said, 'I shall draw water for your camels also until they have had enough.' She quickly emptied her jar into the water trough, and then hurrying again to the well she drew water and watered all the camels.

The man was watching quietly to see whether or not the Lord had made his journey successful, and when the camels had finished drinking, he took a gold nose-ring weighing half a shekel, and two bracelets for her wrists weighing ten shekels, also of gold. 'Tell me, please, whose daughter you are,' he said. 'Is there room in your father's house for us to spend the night?' She answered, 'I am the daughter of Bethuel son of Nahor and Milcah; we have plenty of straw and fodder and also room for you to spend the night.' So the man bowed down and prostrated himself before the Lord and said, 'Blessed be the Lord the God of my master Abraham. His faithfulness to my master has been constant and unfailing, for he has guided me to the house of my master's kinsman.'

The girl ran to her mother's house and told them what had happened. Rebecca had a brother named Laban, and, when he saw the nose-ring, and also the bracelets on his sister's wrists, and heard his sister Rebecca's account of what the man had said to her, he hurried out to the spring. When he got there he found the man still standing by the camels. 'Come in,' he said, 'you whom the Lord has blessed. Why are you staying out here? I have prepared the house and there is a place for the camels.' The man went into the house, while the camels were unloaded and provided with straw and fodder, and water was brought for him and his men to bathe their feet. But when food was set before him, he protested, 'I will not eat until I have delivered my message.' Laban said, 'Let us hear it.'

'I am Abraham's servant,' he answered. 'The Lord has greatly blessed my master, and he has become a wealthy man: the Lord has given him flocks and herds, silver and gold, male and female slaves, camels and donkeys. My master's wife Sarah in her old age bore him a son, to whom he has assigned all that he has. My master made me swear an oath, saying, "You must not take a wife for my son from the women of the Canaanites in whose land I am living; but go to my father's home, to my family, to get a wife for him." I asked, "What if the woman will not come with me?" He answered, "The Lord, in whose presence I have lived, will send his angel with you and make your journey successful. You are to take a wife for my son from my family and from my father's house; then you will be released from the charge I have laid upon you. But if, when you come to my family, they refuse to give her to you, you will likewise be released from the charge."

'Today when I came to the spring, I prayed, "Lord God of my master Abraham, if you will make my journey successful, let it turn out in this way: here I am by the spring; when a young woman comes out to draw water, I shall say to her, 'Give me a little water from your jar to drink.' If she answers, 'Yes, do drink, and I shall draw water for your camels as well,' she is the woman whom the Lord intends for my master's son." Before I had finished praying, I saw Rebecca coming out with her water-jar on her shoulder. She went down to the spring and drew water, and I said to her, "Will you please give me a drink?" At once she lowered her jar from her shoulder and said, "Drink; and I shall also water your camels." So I drank, and she also gave the camels water. I asked her whose daughter she was, and she said, "I am the daughter of Bethuel son of Nahor and Milcah." Then I put the ring in her nose and the bracelets on her wrists, and I bowed low in worship before the Lord. I blessed the Lord, the God of my master Abraham, who had led me by the right road to take my master's niece for his son. Now tell me if you mean to deal loyally and faithfully with my master. If not, say so, and I shall turn elsewhere.'

Laban and Bethuel replied, 'Since this is from the Lord, we can say nothing for or against it. Here is Rebecca; take her and go. She shall be the wife of your master's son, as the Lord has decreed.' When Abraham's servant heard what they said, he prostrated himself on the ground before the Lord. Then he brought out silver and gold ornaments, and articles of clothing, and gave them to Rebecca, and he gave costly gifts to her brother and her mother. He and his men then ate and drank and spent the night there.

When they rose in the morning, Abraham's servant said, 'Give me leave to go back to my master.' Rebecca's brother and her mother replied, 'Let the girl stay with us for a few days, say ten days, and then she can go.' But he said to them, 'Do not detain me, for it is the Lord who has granted me success. Give me leave to go back to my master.' They said, 'Let us call the girl and see what she says.' They called Rebecca and asked her if she would go with the man, and she answered, 'Yes, I will go.' So they let their sister Rebecca and her maid go with Abraham's servant and his men. They blessed Rebecca and said to her:

> You are our sister, may you be the mother of many children;
> may your sons possess the cities of their enemies.

Rebecca and her companions mounted their camels to follow the man. So the servant took Rebecca and set out.

Isaac meanwhile had moved on as far as Beer-lahai-roi and was living in the Negeb. One evening when he had gone out into the open country hoping to meet them, he looked and saw camels approaching. When Rebecca saw Isaac, she dismounted from her camel, saying to the servant, 'Who is that man walking across the open country towards us?' When the servant answered, 'It is my master,' she took her veil and covered herself. The servant related to Isaac all that had happened. Isaac conducted her into the tent and took her as his wife. So she became his wife, and he loved her and was consoled for the death of his mother.

THE DEATH OF ABRAHAM
Genesis 25:5–11

Abraham had assigned all that he possessed to Isaac; and he had already in his lifetime made gifts to his sons by his concubines and had sent them away eastwards, to a land of the east, out of his son Isaac's way. Abraham had lived for a hundred and seventy-five years when he breathed his last. He died at a great age, a full span of years, and was gathered to his forefathers. His sons, Isaac and Ishmael, buried him in the cave at Machpelah, on the land of Ephron son of

Zohar the Hittite, east of Mamre, the plot which Abraham had bought from the Hittites. There Abraham was buried with his wife Sarah. After the death of Abraham, God blessed his son Isaac, who settled close by Beer-lahai-roi.

Part Three

Jacob and Esau

ESAU SELLS HIS BIRTHRIGHT
Genesis 25:21–34

Isaac appealed to the Lord on behalf of his wife because she was childless; the Lord gave heed to his entreaty, and Rebecca conceived. The children pressed on each other in her womb, and she said, 'If all is well, why am I like this?' She went to seek guidance of the Lord, who said to her:

> Two nations are in your womb,
> two peoples going their own ways from birth.
> One will be stronger than the other;
> the elder will be servant to the younger.

When her time had come, there were indeed twins in her womb. The first to come out was reddish and covered with hairs like a cloak, and they named him Esau. Immediately afterwards his brother was born with his hand grasping Esau's heel, and he was given the name Jacob. Isaac was sixty years old when they were born.

As the boys grew up, Esau became a skilful hunter, an outdoor man, while Jacob lived quietly among the tents. Isaac favoured Esau because he kept him supplied with game, but Rebecca favoured Jacob. One day Jacob was preparing broth when Esau came in from the country, exhausted. He said to Jacob, 'I am exhausted; give me a helping of that red broth.' This is why he was called Edom. Jacob retorted, 'Not till you sell me your rights as the firstborn.' Esau replied, 'Here I am at death's door; what use is a birthright to me?' Jacob said, 'First give me your oath!' So he gave him his oath and sold his birthright to Jacob. Then Jacob gave Esau bread and some lentil broth, and he ate and drank and went his way...

JACOB DISPOSSESSES ESAU
Genesis 27:1 – 28:4

When Isaac grew old and his eyes had become so dim that he could not see, he called for his elder son Esau. 'My son!' he said. Esau answered, 'Here I am.' Isaac said, 'Listen now: I am old and I do not know when I may die. Take your hunting gear, your quiver and bow, and go out into the country and get me some game. Then make me a savoury dish, the kind I like, and bring it for me to eat so that I may give you my blessing before I die.'

Now Rebecca had been listening as Isaac talked to his son Esau. When Esau went off into the country to hunt game for his father, she said to her son Jacob, 'I have just overheard your father say to your brother Esau, "Bring me some game and make a savoury dish for me to eat so that I may bless you in the presence of the Lord before I die." Listen now to me, my son, and do what I tell you. Go to the flock and pick me out two fine young kids, and I shall make them into a savoury dish for your father, the kind he likes. Then take it in to your father to eat so that he may bless you before he dies.' 'But my brother Esau is a hairy man,' Jacob said to his mother Rebecca, 'and my skin is smooth. Suppose my father touches me; he will know that I am playing a trick on him and I shall bring a curse instead of a blessing on myself.' His mother answered, 'Let any curse for you fall on me, my son. Do as I say; go and fetch me the kids.'

So Jacob went and got them and brought them to his mother, who made them into a savoury dish such as his father liked. Rebecca then took her elder son's clothes, Esau's best clothes which she had by her in the house, and put them on Jacob her younger son. She put the goatskins on his hands and on the smooth nape of his neck. Then she handed to her son Jacob the savoury dish and the bread she had made.

He went in to his father and said, 'Father!' Isaac answered, 'Yes, my son; which are you?' Jacob answered, 'I am Esau, your elder son. I have done as you told me. Come, sit up and eat some of the game I have for you and then give me your blessing.' Isaac said, 'How did you find it so quickly, my son?' Jacob answered, 'Because the Lord your God put it in my way.' Isaac then said to Jacob, 'Come close and let me touch you, my son, to make sure that you are my son Esau.' When

Jacob came close to his father, Isaac felt him and said, 'The voice is Jacob's voice, but the hands are the hands of Esau.' He did not recognize him, because his hands were hairy like Esau's, and so he blessed him.

He asked, 'Are you really my son Esau?' and when he answered, 'Yes, I am,' Isaac said, 'Bring me some of the game to eat, my son, so that I may give you my blessing.' Jacob brought it to him, and he ate; he brought him wine also, and he drank it. Then his father said to him, 'Come near, my son, and kiss me.' So he went near and kissed him, and when Isaac smelt the smell of his clothes, he blessed him and said, 'The smell of my son is like the smell of open country blessed by the Lord.

> 'God give you dew from heaven
> and the richness of the earth,
> corn and new wine in plenty!
> May peoples serve you
> and nations bow down to you.
> May you be lord over your brothers,
> and may your mother's sons bow down to you.
> A curse on those who curse you,
> but a blessing on those who bless you!'

Isaac finished blessing Jacob, who had scarcely left his father's presence when his brother Esau came in from hunting. He too prepared a savoury dish and brought it to his father. He said, 'Come, father, eat some of the game I have for you, and then give me your blessing.' 'Who are you?' his father Isaac asked him. 'I am Esau, your elder son,' he replied. Then Isaac, greatly agitated, said, 'Then who was it that hunted game and brought it to me? I ate it just before you came in, and I blessed him, and the blessing will stand.' When Esau heard this, he lamented loudly and bitterly. 'Father, bless me too,' he begged. But Isaac said, 'Your brother came full of deceit and took your blessing.' 'He is not called Jacob for nothing,' said Esau. 'This is the second time he has supplanted me. He took away my right as the firstborn, and now he has taken away my blessing. Have you kept back any blessing for me?' Isaac answered, 'I have made him lord over you and set all his brothers under him. I have bestowed upon him grain and new wine for his sustenance. What is there left that I can do for you, my son?' Esau asked, 'Had you then only one blessing, father? Bless me, too, my father.' Esau wept bitterly, and his father Isaac answered:

> Your dwelling will be far from the richness of the earth,
> far from the dew of heaven above.
> By your sword you will live,
> and you will serve your brother.
> But the time will come when you grow restive
> and break his yoke from your neck.

Esau harboured a grudge against Jacob because of the blessing which his father had given him, and he said to himself, 'The time of mourning for my father will soon be here; then I am going to kill my brother Jacob.' When Rebecca was told what her elder son Esau was planning, she called Jacob, her younger son, and said to him, 'Your brother Esau is threatening to kill you. Now, my son, listen to me. Be off at once to my brother Laban in Harran, and stay with him for a while until your brother's anger cools. When it has died down and he has forgotten what you did to him, I will send and fetch you back. Why should I lose you both in one day?'

Rebecca said to Isaac, 'I am weary to death of Hittite women! If Jacob marries a Hittite woman like those who live here, my life will not be worth living.' So Isaac called Jacob, and after blessing him, gave him these instructions: 'You are not to marry a Canaanite woman. Go now to the home of Bethuel, your mother's father, in Paddan-aram, and there find a wife, one of the daughters of Laban, your mother's brother. May God Almighty bless you; may he make you fruitful and increase your descendants until they become a community of nations. May he bestow on you and your offspring the blessing given to Abraham, that you may possess the land where you are now living, and which God assigned to Abraham!'

JACOB'S LADDER
Genesis 28:10–19

Jacob set out from Beersheba and journeyed towards Harran. He came to a certain shrine and, because the sun had gone down, he stopped for the night. He took one of the stones there and, using it as a pillow under his head, he lay down to sleep. In a dream he saw a ladder, which rested on the ground with its top reaching to heaven, and angels of God were going up and down on it. The Lord was standing beside him saying, 'I am the Lord, the God of your father Abraham and the God of Isaac. This land on which you are lying I shall give to you and your descendants. They will be countless as the specks of dust on the ground, and you will spread far and wide, to west and east, to north and south. All the families of the earth will wish to be blessed as you and your descendants are blessed. I shall be with you to protect you wherever you go, and I shall bring you back to this land. I shall not leave you until I have done what I have promised you.'

When Jacob woke from his sleep he said, 'Truly the Lord is in this place, and I did not know it.' He was awestruck and said, 'How awesome is this place! This is none other than the house of God; it is the gateway to heaven.' Early in the morning, when Jacob awoke, he took the stone on which his head had rested, and set it up as a sacred pillar, pouring oil over it. He named that place Beth-el; but the earlier name of the town was Luz.

JACOB AND HIS WIVES
Genesis 29:1 – 30:5, 22–24

Jacob, continuing his journey, came to the land of the eastern tribes. There he saw a well in the open country with three flocks of sheep lying beside it, because flocks were watered from that well. Over its mouth was a huge stone, and all the herdsmen used to gather there and roll it off the mouth of the well and water the flocks; then they would replace the stone over the well.

Jacob said to them, 'Where are you from, my friends?' 'We are from Harran,' they replied. He asked them if they knew Laban the grandson of Nahor. They answered, 'Yes, we do.' 'Is he well?' Jacob asked; and they answered, 'Yes, he is well, and there is his daughter Rachel coming with the flock.' Jacob said, 'It is still broad daylight, and not yet time for penning the sheep. Water the flocks and then go and let them graze.' But they replied, 'We cannot, until all the herdsmen have assembled and the stone has been rolled away from the mouth of the well; then we can water our flocks.' While he was talking to them, Rachel arrived with her father's flock, for she was a shepherdess. Immediately Jacob saw Rachel, the daughter of Laban his mother's brother, with Laban's flock, he went forward, rolled the stone off the mouth of the well and watered Laban's sheep. He kissed Rachel, and was moved to tears. When he told her that he was her father's kinsman, Rebecca's son, she ran and told her father. No sooner had Laban heard the news of his sister's son Jacob, than he hurried to meet him, embraced and kissed him, and welcomed him to his home. Jacob told Laban all that had happened, and Laban said, 'Yes, you are my own flesh and blood.'

After Jacob had stayed with him for a whole month, Laban said to him, 'Why should you work for me for nothing simply because you are my kinsman? Tell me what wage you would settle for.' Now Laban had two daughters: the elder was called Leah, and the younger Rachel. Leah was dull-eyed, but Rachel was beautiful in both face and figure, and Jacob had fallen in love with her. He said, 'For your younger daughter Rachel I would work seven years.' Laban replied, 'It is better that I should give her to you than to anyone else; stay with me.'

When Jacob had worked seven years for Rachel, and they seemed like a few days because he loved her, he said to Laban, 'I have served my time. Give me my wife that I may lie with her.' Laban brought all the people of the place together and held a wedding feast. In the evening he took his daughter Leah and brought her to Jacob, and he lay with her. At the same time Laban gave his slave-girl Zilpah to his daughter Leah. But when morning came, there was Leah! Jacob said to Laban, 'What is this you have done to me? It was for Rachel I worked. Why have you played this trick on me?' Laban answered, 'It is against the custom of our country to marry off the younger sister before the elder. Go through with the seven days' feast for the elder, and the younger shall be given you in return for a further seven years' work.' Jacob agreed, and completed the seven days for Leah.

Then Laban gave Jacob his daughter Rachel to be his wife; and to serve Rachel he gave his slave-girl Bilhah. Jacob lay with Rachel also; he loved her rather than Leah, and he worked for Laban for a further seven years. When the Lord saw that Leah was unloved, he granted her a child, but Rachel remained childless. Leah conceived and gave birth to a son; and she called him Reuben, for she said, 'The Lord has seen my humiliation, but now my husband will love me.' Again she conceived and had a son and said, 'The Lord, hearing that I am unloved, has given me this child also'; and she called him Simeon. She conceived again and had a son and said, 'Now that I have borne him three sons my husband will surely be attached to me.' So she called him Levi. Once more she conceived and had a son, and said, 'Now I shall praise the Lord'; therefore she named him Judah. Then for a while she bore no more children.

When Rachel found that she bore Jacob no children, she became jealous of her sister and complained to Jacob, 'Give me sons, or I shall die!' Jacob said angrily to Rachel, 'Can I take the place of God, who has denied you children?' 'Here is my slave-girl Bilhah,' she replied. 'Lie with her, so that she may bear sons to be laid upon my knees, and through her I too may build up a family.' When she gave him her slave-girl Bilhah as a wife, Jacob lay with her, and she conceived and bore him a son...

Then God took thought for Rachel; he heard her prayer and gave her a child. After she conceived and bore a son, she said, 'God has taken away my humiliation.' She named him Joseph, saying, 'May the Lord add another son to me!'

THE ESCAPE FROM LABAN
Genesis 30:25–43; 31:1–3, 17–46, 51–55

After Rachel had given birth to Joseph, Jacob said to Laban, 'Send me on my way, for I want to return to my own home and country. Give me my wives and children for whom I have served you, and I shall go; you know what service I have rendered you.'

Laban answered, 'I should like to say this – I have become prosperous and the Lord has blessed me through you. So now tell me what wages I owe you, and I shall give you them.'

'You know how I have served you,' replied Jacob, 'and how your herds have prospered under my care. The few you had when I came have increased beyond measure, and wherever I went the Lord brought you blessings. But is it not time for me to make provision for my family?'

Laban said, 'Then what shall I give you?'

'Nothing at all,' answered Jacob; 'I will tend your flocks and be in charge of them as before, if you will do what I suggest. I shall go through your flocks today and pick out from them every black lamb, and all the brindled and the spotted goats, and they will be my wages. This is a fair offer, and it will be to my own disadvantage later on, when we come to settling my wages: any goat amongst mine that is not spotted or brindled and any lamb that is not black will have been stolen.'

Laban agreed: 'Let it be as you say.' But that same day Laban removed the he-goats that were striped and brindled and all the spotted and brindled she-goats, all that had any white on them, and every ram that was black, and he handed them over to his sons. Then he put a distance of three days' journey between himself and Jacob, while Jacob was tending the rest of Laban's flocks.

So Jacob took fresh rods of poplar, almond, and plane trees, and peeled off strips of bark, exposing the white of the rods. He fixed the peeled rods upright in the troughs at the watering-places where the flocks came to drink, so that they were facing the she-goats that were in heat when they came to drink. They mated beside the rods and gave birth to young that were striped and spotted and brindled. The rams Jacob separated, and let the ewes run only with such of the rams in Laban's flocks as were striped and black; and thus he built up flocks for himself, which he did not add to Laban's sheep. As for the goats, whenever the more vigorous were in heat, he set the rods in front of them at the troughs so that they mated beside the rods. He did not put them there for the weaker goats, and in this way the weaker came to be Laban's and the stronger Jacob's. So Jacob's wealth increased more and more until he possessed great flocks, as well as male and female slaves, camels, and donkeys.

Jacob learnt that Laban's sons were saying, 'Jacob has taken everything that our father had, and all his wealth has come from our father's property.' He noticed also that Laban was not so well disposed to him as he had once been. The Lord said to Jacob, 'Go back to the land of your fathers and to your kindred; I shall be with you.'...

At once Jacob put his sons and his wives on camels, and he drove off all the cattle and other livestock which he had acquired in Paddan-aram, to go to his father Isaac in Canaan.

When Laban had gone to shear his sheep, Rachel stole the household gods belonging to her father. Jacob hoodwinked Laban the Aramaean and kept his departure secret; he fled with all that he possessed, and soon was over the Euphrates and on the way to the hill-country of Gilead.

Three days later, when Laban heard that Jacob had fled, he took his kinsmen with him and pursued Jacob for seven days until he caught up with him in the hill-country of Gilead. But God came to Laban the Aramaean in a dream by night and said to him, 'Be careful to say nothing to Jacob, not a word.'

When Laban caught up with him, Jacob had pitched his tent in the hill-country of Gilead, and Laban encamped with his kinsmen in the same hill-country. Laban said to Jacob, 'What have you done? You have deceived me and carried off my daughters as though they were captives taken in war. Why did you slip away secretly without telling me? I would have set you on your way with songs and the music of tambourines and harps. You did not even let me kiss my daughters and their children. In this you behaved foolishly. I have it in my power to harm all of you, but last night the God of your father spoke to me; he told me to be careful to say nothing to you, not one word. I expect that really you went away because you were homesick and pining for your father's house; but why did you steal my gods?'

Jacob answered, 'I was afraid; I thought you would take your daughters from me by force. Whoever is found in possession of your gods shall die for it. In the presence of our kinsmen as witnesses, identify anything I have that is yours, and take it back.' Jacob did not know that Rachel had stolen the gods. Laban went into Jacob's tent and Leah's tent and that of the two slave-girls, but he found nothing. After coming from Leah's tent he went into Rachel's. In the mean time Rachel had taken the household gods and put them in the camel-bag and was sitting on them. Laban went through the whole tent but found nothing. Rachel said, 'Do not take it amiss, father, that I cannot rise in your presence: the common lot of woman is upon me.' So for all his searching, Laban did not find the household gods.

Jacob heatedly took Laban to task. 'What have I done wrong?' he exclaimed. 'What is my offence, that you have come after me in hot pursuit and have gone through all my belongings? Have you found a single article belonging to your household? If so, set it here in front of my kinsmen and yours, and let them decide between the two of us. In all the twenty years I have been with you, your ewes and she-goats have never miscarried. I have never eaten rams from your flocks. I have never brought to you the carcass of any animal mangled by wild beasts, but I bore the loss myself. You demanded that I should pay compensation for anything stolen by day or by night. This was the way of it: the heat wore me down by day and the frost by night; I got no sleep. For twenty years I have been in your household. I worked fourteen years for you to win your two daughters and six years for your flocks, and you changed my wages ten times over. If the God of my father, the God of Abraham and the Fear of Isaac, had not been with me, you would now have sent me away empty-handed. But God saw my labour and my hardships, and last night he delivered his verdict.'

Laban answered Jacob, 'The daughters are my daughters, the children are my children, the flocks are my flocks; all you see is mine. But what am I to do now about my daughters and the children they have borne? Come, let us make a pact, you and I, and let there be a witness between us.' So Jacob chose a great stone and set it up as a sacred pillar. Then he told his kinsmen to gather stones, and they took them and built a cairn, and there beside the cairn they ate together...

Laban said to Jacob, 'Here is this cairn, and here the pillar which I have set up between us. Both cairn and pillar are witnesses that I am not to pass beyond this cairn to your side with evil intent, and you must not pass beyond this cairn and this pillar to my side with evil intent. May the God of Abraham and the God of Nahor judge between us.' Jacob swore this oath in the name of the Fear of Isaac, the God of his father. He slaughtered an animal for sacrifice there in the hill-country, and summoned his kinsmen to the feast. They ate together and spent the night there.

Laban rose early in the morning, kissed his daughters and their children, gave them his blessing, and then returned to his home.

JACOB PREPARES TO MEET ESAU
Genesis 32:1–21

As Jacob continued his journey he was met by angels of God. When he saw them, Jacob exclaimed, 'This is the company of God,' and he called that place Mahanaim.

Jacob sent messengers ahead of him to his brother Esau to the district of Seir in Edomite territory, instructing them to say to Esau, 'My lord, your servant Jacob sends this message: I have been living with Laban and have stayed there till now. I have acquired oxen, donkeys, and sheep, as well as male and female slaves, and I am sending to tell you this, my lord, so that I may win your favour.' The messengers returned to Jacob and said, 'We went to your brother Esau and he is already on the way to meet you with four hundred men.' Jacob, much afraid and distressed, divided the people with him, as well as the sheep, cattle, and camels, into two companies. He reasoned that, if Esau should come upon one company and destroy it, the other might still survive.

Jacob prayed, 'God of my father Abraham, God of my father Isaac, Lord at whose bidding I came back to my own country and to my kindred, and who promised me prosperity, I am not worthy of all the true and steadfast love which you have shown to me your servant. The last time I crossed the Jordan, I owned nothing but the staff in my hand; now I have two camps. Save me, I pray, from my brother Esau, for I am afraid that he may come and destroy me; he will spare neither mother nor child. But you said, "I shall make you prosper and your descendants will be like the sand of the sea, beyond all counting."'

After spending the night there Jacob chose a gift for his brother Esau from the herds he had with him: two hundred she-goats, twenty he-goats, two hundred ewes and twenty rams, thirty milch-camels with their young, forty cows and ten young bulls, twenty she-donkeys and ten donkeys. He put each drove into the charge of a servant and said, 'Go on ahead of me, and leave gaps between one drove and the next.' To the first servant he gave these instructions: 'When my brother Esau meets you and asks who your master is and where you are going and who owns these animals you are driving, you are to say, "They belong to your servant Jacob, who sends them as a gift to my lord Esau; he himself is coming behind us."' He gave the same instructions to the second, to the third, and to all the drovers, telling each to say the same thing to Esau when they met him. And they were to add, 'Your servant Jacob is coming behind us.' Jacob thought, 'I shall appease him with the gift that I have sent on ahead, and afterwards, when we come face to face, perhaps he will receive me kindly.' So Jacob's gift went on ahead of him, while he himself stayed that night at Mahaneh.

WRESTLING WITH GOD
Genesis 32:22–32

During the night Jacob rose, and taking his two wives, his two slave-girls, and his eleven sons, he crossed the ford of Jabbok. After he had sent them across the wadi with all that he had, Jacob was left alone, and a man wrestled with him there till daybreak. When the man saw that he could not get the better of Jacob, he struck him in the hollow of his thigh, so that Jacob's hip was dislocated as they wrestled. The man said, 'Let me go, for day is breaking,' but Jacob replied, 'I will not let you go unless you bless me.' The man asked, 'What is your name?' 'Jacob,' he answered. The man said, 'Your name shall no longer be Jacob but Israel, because you have striven with God and with mortals, and have prevailed.' Jacob said, 'Tell me your name, I pray.' He replied, 'Why do you ask my name?' but he gave him his blessing there. Jacob called the place Peniel, 'because', he said, 'I have seen God face to face yet my life is spared'.

The sun rose as Jacob passed through Penuel, limping because of his hip. That is why to this day the Israelites do not eat the sinew that is on the hollow of the thigh, because the man had struck Jacob on that sinew.

A MEETING AND A PARTING
Genesis 33

Jacob looked up and there was Esau coming with four hundred men. He divided the children between Leah and Rachel and the two slave-girls. He put the slave-girls and their children in front, Leah with her children next, and Rachel and Joseph in the rear. He himself went on ahead of them, bowing low to the ground seven times as he approached his brother. Esau ran to meet him and embraced him; he threw his arms round him and kissed him, and they both wept.

When Esau caught sight of the women and children, he asked, 'Who are these with you?' Jacob replied, 'The children whom God has graciously given to your servant.' The slave-girls came near, each with her children, and they bowed low; then Leah with her children came near and bowed low, and lastly Joseph and Rachel came and bowed low also. Esau asked, 'What was all that company of yours that I met?' 'It was meant to win favour with you, my lord,' was the answer. Esau said, 'I have more than enough. Keep what you have, my brother.' But Jacob replied, 'No, please! If I have won your favour, then accept, I pray, this gift from me; for, as you see, I come into your presence as into that of a god, and yet you receive me favourably. Accept this gift which I bring you; for God has been gracious to me, and I have all I want.' Thus urged, Esau accepted it.

Esau said, 'Let us set out, and I shall go at your pace.' But Jacob answered him, 'You must know, my lord, that the children are small; the flocks and herds are suckling their young and I am concerned for them, and if they are overdriven for a single day, my beasts will all die. I beg you, my lord, to go on ahead, and I shall move by easy stages at the pace of the livestock I am driving and the pace of the children, until I come to my lord in Seir.' Esau said, 'Let me detail some of my men to escort you,' but he replied, 'There is no reason why my lord should be so kind.' That day Esau turned back towards Seir, while Jacob set out for Succoth; there he built himself a house and made shelters for his cattle. Therefore he named that place Succoth.

So having journeyed from Paddan-aram, Jacob arrived safely at the town of Shechem in Canaan and pitched his tent to the east of it. The piece of land where he had pitched his tent he bought from the sons of Hamor, Shechem's father, for a hundred sheep. He erected an altar there and called it El-elohey-israel.

THE RAPE OF DINAH
Genesis 34

Dinah, the daughter whom Leah had borne to Jacob, went out to visit women of the district, and Shechem, son of Hamor the Hivite, the local prince, saw her. He took her, lay with her, and violated her. But Shechem was deeply attached to Jacob's daughter Dinah; he loved the girl and sought to win her affection. Shechem said to Hamor his father, 'You must get me this girl as my wife.' When Jacob learnt that his daughter Dinah had been dishonoured, his sons were with the herds in the open country, so he held his peace until they came home. Meanwhile Shechem's father Hamor came out to Jacob to talk the matter over with him. When they heard the news Jacob's sons came home from the country; they were distressed and very angry, because in lying with Jacob's daughter Shechem had done what the Israelites hold to be an intolerable outrage. Hamor appealed to them: 'My son Shechem is in love with this girl; I beg you to let him have her as his wife. Let us ally ourselves in marriage; you give us your daughters, and you take ours. If you settle among us, the country is open before you; make your home in it, move about freely, and acquire land of your own.' Shechem said to the girl's father and brothers, 'I am eager to win your favour and I shall give whatever you ask. Fix the bride-price and the gift as high as you like, and I shall give whatever you ask; only, give me the girl in marriage.'

Jacob's sons replied to Shechem and his father Hamor deceitfully, because Shechem had violated their sister Dinah: 'We cannot do this,' they said; 'we cannot give our sister to a man who is uncircumcised, for we look on that as a disgrace. Only on one condition can we give our consent: if you follow our example and have every male among you circumcised, we shall give you our daughters and take yours for ourselves. We will then live among you, and become one people with you. But if you refuse to listen to us and be circumcised, we shall take the girl and go.' Their proposal appeared satisfactory to Hamor and his son Shechem; and the young man, who was held in respect above anyone in his father's house, did not hesitate to do what they had said, because his heart had been captured by Jacob's daughter.

Hamor and Shechem went to the gate of their town and addressed their fellow-townsmen: 'These men are friendly towards us,' they said; 'let them live in our country and move freely in it. The land has room enough for them. Let us marry their daughters and give them ours. But on this condition only will these men agree to live with us as one people: every male among us must be circumcised as they are. Their herds, their livestock, and all their chattels will then be ours. We need only agree to their condition, and then they are free to live with us.' All the able-bodied men agreed with Hamor and his son Shechem, and every able-bodied male among them was circumcised. Then two days later, while they were still in pain, two of Jacob's sons, Simeon and Levi, full brothers to Dinah, after arming themselves with swords, boldly entered the town and killed every male. They cut down Hamor and his son Shechem and took Dinah from Shechem's house and went off. Jacob's other sons came in over the dead bodies and plundered the town which had brought dishonour on their sister. They seized flocks, cattle, donkeys, whatever was inside the town and outside in the open country; they carried off all the wealth, the women, and the children, and looted everything in the houses.

Jacob said to Simeon and Levi, 'You have brought trouble on me; you have brought my name into bad odour among the people of the country, the Canaanites and the Perizzites. My numbers are few; if they combine against me and attack, I shall be destroyed, I and my household with me.' They answered, 'Is our sister to be treated as a common whore?'

JACOB RETURNS TO BETHEL
Genesis 35:1–4, 9–29

God said to Jacob, 'Go up now to Bethel and, when you have settled there, erect an altar to the God who appeared to you when you fled from your brother Esau.' Jacob said to his household and to all who were with him, 'Get rid of the foreign gods which you have; then purify yourselves, and put on fresh clothes. We are to set off for Bethel, so that I can erect an altar there to the God who answered me when I was in distress; he has been with me wherever I have gone.'

They handed over to Jacob all the foreign gods in their possession and the ear-rings they were wearing, and he buried them under the terebinth tree near Shechem...

God appeared again to Jacob after his return from Paddan-aram and blessed him. God said: 'Jacob is now your name, but it is going to be Jacob no longer: your name is to be Israel.'

So Jacob was called Israel. God said to him:

'I am God Almighty.
Be fruitful and increase:
a nation, a host of nations will come from you;
kings also will descend from you.
The land I gave to Abraham and Isaac I give to you;
and to your descendants also I shall give this land.'

When God left him, Jacob raised a sacred pillar of stone in the place where God had spoken with him, and he offered a drink-offering on it and poured oil over it. Jacob called the place where God had spoken with him Bethel.

They moved from Bethel, and when there was still some distance to go to Ephrathah, Rachel went into labour and her pains were severe. While they were on her, the midwife said, 'Do not be afraid, for this is another son for you.' Then with her last breath, as she was dying, she named him Ben-oni, but his father called him Benjamin. So Rachel died and was buried by the side of the road to Ephrathah, that is Bethlehem. Over her grave Jacob set up a sacred pillar; and to this day it is known as the Pillar of Rachel's Grave. Then continuing his journey Israel pitched his tent on the other side of Migdal-eder.

While Israel was living in that district, Reuben lay with his father's concubine Bilhah; and Israel came to hear of it.

The sons of Jacob were twelve. The sons of Leah: Jacob's firstborn Reuben, then Simeon, Levi, Judah, Issachar, and Zebulun. The sons of Rachel: Joseph and Benjamin. The sons of Rachel's slave-girl Bilhah: Dan and Naphtali. The sons of Leah's slave-girl Zilpah: Gad and Asher. These were Jacob's sons, born to him in Paddan-aram.

Jacob came to his father Isaac at Mamre near Kiriath-arba, that is Hebron, where Abraham and Isaac had stayed. Isaac was a hundred and eighty years old when he breathed his last. He died and was gathered to his father's kin at this very great age, and his sons Esau and Jacob buried him.

Part Four

Joseph and His Brothers

SOLD INTO SLAVERY
Genesis 37

Jacob settled in Canaan, the country in which his father had made his home, and this is an account of Jacob's descendants.

When Joseph was a youth of seventeen, he used to accompany his brothers, the sons of Bilhah and Zilpah, his father's wives, when they were in charge of the flock, and he told tales about them to their father. Because Joseph was a child of his old age, Israel loved him best of all his sons, and he made him a long robe with sleeves. When his brothers saw that their father loved him best, it aroused their hatred and they had nothing but harsh words for him.

Joseph had a dream, and when he told it to his brothers, their hatred of him became still greater. He said to them, 'Listen to this dream I had. We were out in the field binding sheaves, when all at once my sheaf rose and stood upright, and your sheaves gathered round and bowed in homage before my sheaf.' His brothers retorted, 'Do you think that you will indeed be king over us and rule us?' and they hated him still more because of his dreams and what he had said. Then he had another dream, which he related to his father and his brothers. 'Listen!' he said. 'I have had another dream, and in it the sun, the moon, and eleven stars were bowing down to me.' When he told his father and his brothers, his father took him to task: 'What do you mean by this dream of yours?' he asked. 'Are we to come and bow to the ground before you, I and your mother and your brothers?' His brothers were jealous of him, but his father did not forget the incident.

Joseph's brothers had gone to herd their father's flocks at Shechem. Israel said to him, 'Your brothers are herding the flocks at Shechem; I am going to send you to them.' Joseph answered, 'I am ready to go.' Israel told him to go and see if all was well with his brothers and the flocks, and to bring back word to him. So Joseph was sent off from the vale of Hebron and came to Shechem, where a man met him wandering in the open country and asked him what he was looking for. 'I am looking for my brothers,' he replied. 'Can you tell me where they are herding the flocks?' The man said, 'They have moved from here; I heard them speak of going to Dothan.' Joseph went after his brothers and came up with them at Dothan. They saw him in the distance, and before he reached them, they plotted to kill him. 'Here comes that dreamer,' they said to one another. 'Now is our chance; let us kill him and throw him into one of these cisterns; we can say that a wild beast has devoured him. Then we shall see what becomes of his dreams.' When Reuben heard, he came to his rescue, urging them not to take his life. 'Let us have no bloodshed,' he said. 'Throw him into this cistern in the wilderness, but do him no injury.' Reuben meant to rescue him from their clutches in order to restore him to his father. When Joseph reached his brothers, they stripped him of the long robe with sleeves which he was wearing, picked him up, and threw him into the cistern. It was empty, with no water in it.

They had sat down to eat when, looking up, they saw an Ishmaelite caravan coming from Gilead on the way down to Egypt, with camels carrying gum tragacanth and balm and myrrh. Judah said to his brothers, 'What do we gain by killing our brother and concealing his death? Why not sell him to these Ishmaelites? Let us do him no harm, for after all, he is our brother, our own flesh and blood'; his brothers agreed. Meanwhile some passing Midianite merchants drew Joseph up out of the cistern and sold him for twenty pieces of silver to the Ishmaelites; they brought Joseph to Egypt. When Reuben came back to the cistern, he found Joseph had gone. He tore his clothes and going to his brothers he said, 'The boy is not there. Whatever shall I do?'

Joseph's brothers took the long robe with sleeves, and dipped it in the blood of a goat which they had killed. After tearing the robe, they brought it to their father and said, 'Look what we have found. Do you recognize it? Is this your son's robe or not?' Jacob recognized it. 'It is my son's,' he said. 'A wild beast has devoured him. Joseph has been torn to pieces.' Jacob tore his clothes; he put on sackcloth and for many days he mourned his son. Though his sons and daughters all tried to comfort him, he refused to be comforted. He said, 'No, I shall go to Sheol mourning for my son.' Thus Joseph's father wept for him. The Midianites meanwhile had sold Joseph in Egypt to Potiphar, one of Pharaoh's court officials, the captain of the guard.

TAMAR PLAYS THE HARLOT
Genesis 38:1–26

About that time Judah parted from his brothers, and heading south he pitched his tent in company with an Adullamite named Hirah. There he saw Bathshua the daughter of a Canaanite and married her. He lay with her, and she conceived and bore a son, whom she called Er. She conceived again and bore a son, whom she called Onan. Once more she conceived and bore a son whom she called Shelah, and she was at Kezib when she bore him. Judah found a wife for his eldest son Er; her name was Tamar. But Judah's eldest son Er was wicked in the Lord's sight, and the Lord took away his life. Then Judah told Onan to sleep with his brother's wife, to do his duty as the husband's brother and raise up offspring for his brother. But Onan knew that the offspring would not count as his; so whenever he lay with his brother's wife, he spilled his seed on the ground so as not to raise up offspring for his brother. What he did was wicked in the Lord's sight, and the Lord took away his life also. Judah said to his daughter-in-law Tamar, 'Remain as a widow in your father's house until my son Shelah grows up'; for he was afraid that Shelah too might die like his brothers. So Tamar went and stayed in her father's house.

Time passed, and Judah's wife Bathshua died. When he had finished mourning, he and his friend Hirah the Adullamite went up to Timnath at sheep-shearing. When Tamar was told that her father-in-law was on his way to shear his sheep at Timnath, she took off her widow's clothes, covered her face with a veil, and then sat where the road forks on the way to Timnath. She did this because she saw that although Shelah was now grown up she had not been given to him as a wife. When Judah saw her he thought she was a prostitute, for she had veiled her face. He turned to her where she sat by the roadside

165

and said, 'Let me lie with you,' not realizing she was his daughter-in-law. She said, 'What will you give to lie with me?' He answered, 'I shall send you a young goat from my flock.' She said, 'I agree, if you will give me a pledge until you send it.' He asked what pledge he should give her, and she replied, 'Your seal and its cord, and the staff which you are holding.' He handed them over to her and lay with her, and she became pregnant. She then rose and went home, where she took off her veil and put on her widow's clothes again.

Judah sent the goat by his friend the Adullamite in order to recover the pledge from the woman, but he could not find her. When he enquired of the people of that place, 'Where is that temple-prostitute, the one who was sitting where the road forks?' they answered, 'There has been no temple-prostitute here.' So he went back to Judah and reported that he had failed to find her and that the men of the place had said there was no such prostitute there. Judah said, 'Let her keep the pledge, or we shall be a laughing-stock. After all, I did send the kid, even though you could not find her.'

About three months later Judah was told that his daughter-in-law Tamar had played the prostitute and got herself pregnant. 'Bring her out,' ordered Judah, 'so that she may be burnt.' But as she was being brought out, she sent word to her father-in-law. 'The father of my child is the man to whom these things belong,' she said. 'See if you recognize whose they are, this seal, the pattern of the cord, and the staff.' Judah identified them and said, 'She is more in the right than I am, because I did not give her to my son Shelah.' He did not have intercourse with her again.

POTIPHAR'S WIFE
Genesis 39

When Joseph was taken down to Egypt by the Ishmaelites, he was bought from them by an Egyptian, Potiphar, one of Pharaoh's court officials, the captain of the guard. Joseph prospered, for the Lord was with him. He lived in the house of his Egyptian master, who saw that the Lord was with him and was giving him success in all that he undertook. Thus Joseph won his master's favour, and became his attendant. Indeed, his master put him in charge of his household, and entrusted him with everything he had. From the time that he put Joseph in charge of his household and all his property, the Lord blessed the household through Joseph; the Lord's blessing was on all that was his in house and field. Potiphar left it all in Joseph's care, and concerned himself with nothing but the food he ate.

Now Joseph was handsome in both face and figure, and after a time his master's wife became infatuated with him. 'Come, make love to me,' she said. But Joseph refused. 'Think of my master,' he said; 'he leaves the management of his whole house to me; he has trusted me with all he has. I am as important in this house as he is, and he has withheld nothing from me except you, because you are his wife. How can I do such a wicked thing? It is a sin against God.' Though she kept on at Joseph day after day, he refused to lie with her or be in her company.

One day when he came into the house to see to his duties, and none of the household servants was there indoors, she caught him by his loincloth, saying, 'Come, make love to me,' but he left the loincloth in her hand and ran from the house. When she saw that he had left his loincloth and run out of the house, she called to her servants, 'Look at this! My husband has brought in a Hebrew to bring insult on us. He came in here to rape me, but I gave a loud scream. When he heard me scream and call for help, he ran out, leaving his loincloth behind.' She kept it by her until his master came home, and then she repeated her tale: 'That Hebrew slave you brought in came to my room to make me an object of insult. But when I screamed for help, he ran out of the house, leaving his loincloth behind.'

Joseph's master was furious when he heard his wife's account of what his slave had done to her. He had Joseph seized and thrown into the guardhouse, where the king's prisoners were kept; and there he was confined. But the Lord was with Joseph and kept faith with him, so that he won the favour of the governor of the guardhouse. Joseph was put in charge of the prisoners, and he directed all their work. The governor ceased to concern himself with anything entrusted to Joseph, because the Lord was with him and gave him success in all that he did.

PHARAOH'S DREAMS
Genesis 40 and 41

Some time after these events it happened that the king's cupbearer and the royal baker gave offence to their lord, the king of Egypt. Pharaoh was displeased with his two officials, his chief cupbearer and chief baker, and put them in custody in the house of the captain of the guard, in the guardhouse where Joseph was imprisoned. The captain appointed Joseph as their attendant, and he waited on them.

They had been in prison in the guardhouse for some time, when one night the king's cupbearer and his baker both had dreams, each with a meaning of its own. Coming to them in the morning, Joseph saw that they looked dispirited, and asked these officials in custody with him in his master's house, why they were so downcast that day. They replied, 'We have each had a dream, but there is no one to interpret them.' Joseph said to them, 'All interpretation belongs to God. Why not tell me your dreams?' So the chief cupbearer told Joseph his dream: 'In my dream', he said, 'there was a vine in front of me. On the vine there were three branches, and as soon as it budded, it blossomed and its clusters ripened into grapes. I plucked the grapes and pressed them into Pharaoh's cup which I was holding, and then put the cup into Pharaoh's hand.' Joseph said to him, 'This is the interpretation. The three branches are three days: within three days Pharaoh will raise your head and restore you to your post; then you will put the cup into Pharaoh's hand as you used to do when you were his cupbearer. When things go well with you, remember me and do me the kindness of bringing my case to Pharaoh's notice; help me to get out of this prison. I was carried off by force from the land of the Hebrews, and here I have done nothing to deserve being put into this dungeon.'

When the chief baker saw that the interpretation given by Joseph had been favourable, he said to him, 'I too had a dream, and in my dream there were three baskets of white bread on my head. In the top basket there was every kind of food such as a baker might prepare for Pharaoh, but the birds were eating out of the top basket on my head.' Joseph answered, 'This is the interpretation. The three baskets are three days: within three days Pharaoh will raise your head off your shoulders and hang you on a tree, and the birds of the air will devour the flesh off your bones.'

The third day was Pharaoh's birthday and he gave a banquet for all his officials. He had the chief cupbearer and the chief baker brought up where they were all assembled. The cupbearer was restored to his position, and he put the cup into Pharaoh's hand; but the baker was hanged. All went as Joseph had said in interpreting the dreams for them. The cupbearer, however, did not bear Joseph in mind; he forgot him.

Two years later Pharaoh had a dream: he was standing by the Nile, when there came up from the river seven cows, sleek and fat, and they grazed among the reeds. Presently seven other cows, gaunt and lean, came up from the river, and stood beside the cows on the river bank. The cows that were gaunt and lean devoured the seven cows that were sleek and fat. Then Pharaoh woke up.

He fell asleep again and had a second dream: he saw seven ears of grain, full and ripe, growing on a single stalk. Springing up after them were seven other ears, thin and shrivelled by the east wind. The thin ears swallowed up the seven ears that were full and plump. Then Pharaoh woke up and found it was a dream.

In the morning Pharaoh's mind was so troubled that he summoned all the dream-interpreters and wise men of Egypt, and told them his dreams; but there was no one who could interpret them for him. Then Pharaoh's chief cupbearer spoke up. 'Now I must mention my offences,' he said: 'Pharaoh was angry with his servants, and imprisoned me and the chief baker in the house of the captain of the guard. One night we both had dreams, each requiring its own interpretation. We had with us there a young Hebrew, a slave of the captain of the guard, and when we told him our dreams he interpreted them for us, giving each dream its own interpretation. Things turned out exactly as the dreams had been interpreted to us: I was restored to my post, the other was hanged.'

Pharaoh thereupon sent for Joseph, and they hurriedly brought him out of the dungeon. After he had shaved and changed his clothes, he came in before Pharaoh, who said to him, 'I have had a dream which no one can interpret. I have heard that you can interpret any dream you hear.' Joseph answered, 'Not I, but God, can give an answer which will reassure Pharaoh.' Then Pharaoh said to him: 'In my dream I was standing on the bank of the Nile, when there came up from the river seven cows, fat and sleek, and they grazed among the reeds. After them seven other cows came up that were in poor condition, very gaunt and lean; in all Egypt I have never seen such gaunt creatures. These lean, gaunt cows devoured the first cows, the seven fat ones. They were swallowed up, but no one could have told they were in the bellies of the others, which looked just as gaunt as before. Then I woke up. In another dream I saw seven ears of grain, full and ripe, growing on a single stalk. Springing up after them were seven other ears, blighted, thin, and shrivelled by the east wind. The thin ears swallowed up the seven ripe ears. When I spoke to the dream-interpreters, no one could tell me the meaning.'

Joseph said to Pharaoh, 'Pharaoh's dreams are both the same; God has told Pharaoh what he is about to do. The seven good cows are seven years, and the seven good ears of grain are seven years – it is all one dream. The seven lean and gaunt cows that came up after them are seven years, and so also are the seven empty ears of grain blighted by the east wind; there are going to be seven years of famine. It is as I have told Pharaoh: God has let Pharaoh see what he is about to do. There are to be seven years of bumper harvests throughout Egypt. After them will come seven years of famine; so that the great harvests in Egypt will all be forgotten, and famine will ruin the country. The good years will leave no trace in the land because of the famine that follows, for it will be very severe. That Pharaoh has dreamed this twice means God is firmly resolved on this plan, and very soon he will put it into effect.

'Let Pharaoh now look for a man of vision and wisdom and put him in charge of the country. Pharaoh should take steps to appoint commissioners over the land to take one fifth of the produce of Egypt during the seven years of plenty. They should collect all food produced in the good years that are coming and put the grain under Pharaoh's control as a store of food to be kept in the towns. This food will be a reserve for the country against the seven years of famine which will come on Egypt, and so the country will not be devastated by the famine.'

The plan commended itself both to Pharaoh and to all his

officials, and Pharaoh asked them, 'Could we find another man like this, one so endowed with the spirit of God?' To Joseph he said, 'Since God has made all this known to you, no one has your vision and wisdom. You shall be in charge of my household, and all my people will respect your every word. Only in regard to the throne shall I rank higher than you.' Pharaoh went on, 'I hereby give you authority over the whole land of Egypt.' He took off his signet ring and put it on Joseph's finger; he had him dressed in robes of fine linen, and hung a gold chain round his neck. He mounted him in his viceroy's chariot and men cried 'Make way!' before him. Thus Pharaoh made him ruler over all Egypt and said to him, 'I am the Pharaoh, yet without your consent no one will lift hand or foot throughout Egypt.' Pharaoh named him Zaphenath-paneah, and he gave him as his wife Asenath daughter of Potiphera priest of On. Joseph's authority extended over the whole of Egypt.

Joseph was thirty years old at the time he entered the service of Pharaoh king of Egypt. When he left the royal presence, he made a tour of inspection through the land. During the seven years of plenty when there were abundant harvests, Joseph gathered all the food produced in Egypt then and stored it in the towns, putting in each the food from the surrounding country. He stored the grain in huge quantities; it was like the sand of the sea, so much that he stopped measuring: it was beyond all measure.

Before the years of famine came, two sons were born to Joseph by Asenath daughter of Potiphera priest of On. He named the elder Manasseh, 'for', he said, 'God has made me forget all my troubles and my father's family'. He named the second Ephraim, 'for', he said, 'God has made me fruitful in the land of my hardships'. When the seven years of plenty in Egypt came to an end, the seven years of famine began, as Joseph had predicted. There was famine in every country, but there was food throughout Egypt. When the famine came to be felt through all Egypt, the people appealed to Pharaoh for food and he ordered them to go to Joseph and do whatever he told them. When the whole land was in the grip of famine, Joseph opened all the granaries and sold grain to the Egyptians, for the famine was severe. The whole world came to Egypt to buy grain from Joseph, so severe was the famine everywhere.

JOSEPH'S BROTHERS GO TO EGYPT
Genesis 42:1 – 44:12

When Jacob learnt that there was grain in Egypt, he said to his sons, 'Why do you stand staring at each other? I hear there is grain in Egypt. Go down there, and buy some for us to keep us alive and save us from starving to death.' So ten of Joseph's brothers went down to buy grain from Egypt, but Jacob did not let Joseph's brother Benjamin go with them, for fear that he might come to harm.

Thus the sons of Israel went with everyone else to buy grain because of the famine in Canaan. Now Joseph was governor of the land, and it was he who sold the grain to all its people. Joseph's brothers came and bowed to the ground before him, and when he saw his brothers he recognized them but, pretending not to know them, he greeted them harshly. 'Where do you come from?' he demanded. 'From Canaan to buy food,' they answered. Although Joseph had recognized his brothers, they did not recognize him. He remembered the dreams he had had about them and said, 'You are spies; you have come to spy out the weak points in our defences.' 'No, my lord,' they answered; 'your servants have come to buy food. We are all sons of one man. We are honest men; your servants are not spies.' 'No,' he maintained, 'it is to spy out our weaknesses that you have come.' They said, 'There were twelve of us, my lord, all brothers, sons of one man back in Canaan; the youngest is still with our father, and one is lost.' But Joseph insisted, 'As I have already said to you: you are spies. This is how you will be put to the test: unless your youngest brother comes here, I swear by the life of Pharaoh you shall not leave this place. Send one of your number to fetch your brother; the rest of you will remain in prison. Thus your story will be tested to see whether you are telling the truth. If not, then by the life of Pharaoh you must be spies.' With that he kept them in prison for three days.

On the third day Joseph said to them, 'Do what I say and your lives will be spared, for I am a godfearing man: if you are honest men, only one of you brothers shall be kept in prison, while the rest of you may go and take grain for your starving households; but you must bring your youngest brother to me. In this way your words will be proved true, and you will not die.'

They consented, and among themselves they said, 'No doubt we are being punished because of our brother. We saw his distress when he pleaded with us and we refused to listen. That is why this distress has come on us.' Reuben said, 'Did I not warn you not to do wrong to the boy? But you would not listen, and now his blood is on our heads, and we must pay.' They did not know that Joseph understood, since he had used an interpreter. Joseph turned away from them and wept. Then he went back to speak to them, and took Simeon from among them and had him bound before their eyes. He gave orders to fill their bags with grain, to put each man's silver back into his sack again, and to give them provisions for the journey. After this had been done, they loaded their grain on their donkeys and set off. When they stopped for the night, one of them opened his sack to give feed to his donkey, and there at the top was the silver. He said to his brothers, 'My silver has been returned; here it is in my pack.' Bewildered and trembling, they asked one another, 'What is this that God has done to us?'

When they came to their father Jacob in Canaan, they gave him an account of all that had happened to them. They said: 'The man who is lord of the country spoke harshly to us and made out that we were spies. But we said to him, "We are honest men, we are not spies. There were twelve of us, all brothers, sons of the same father. One has disappeared, and the youngest is with our father in Canaan." Then the man, the lord of the country, said to us, "This is how I shall discover if you are honest men: leave one of your brothers with me, take food for your starving households and go; bring your youngest brother to me, and I shall know that you are honest men and not spies. Then I shall restore your brother to you, and you can move around the country freely."' But on emptying their sacks, each of them found his silver inside, and when they and their father saw the bundles of silver, they were afraid. Their father Jacob said to them, 'You have robbed me of my children. Joseph is lost; Simeon is lost; and now you would take Benjamin. Everything is against me.' Reuben said to his father, 'You may put both my sons to death if I do not bring him back to you. Entrust him to me, and I shall bring him back.' But Jacob said, 'My son must not go with you, for his brother is dead and he alone is left. Should he come to any harm on the journey, you will bring down my grey hairs in sorrow to the grave.'

The famine was still severe in the land. When the grain they had brought from Egypt was all used up, their father said to them, 'Go again and buy some more grain for us to eat.' Judah replied, 'But the man warned us that we must not go into his presence unless our brother was with us. If you let our brother go with us, we will go down and buy you food. But if you will not let him, we cannot go, for the man declared, "You shall not come into my presence unless your brother is with you."' Israel said, 'Why have you treated me so badly by telling the man that you had another brother?' They answered, 'The man questioned us closely about ourselves and our family: "Is your father still alive?" he asked, "Have you a brother?" and we answered his questions. How were we to know he would tell us to bring our brother down?' Judah said to Israel his father, 'Send the boy with me; then we can start at once, and save everyone's life, ours, yours, and those of our children. I shall go surety for him, and you may hold me responsible. If I do not bring him back and restore him to you, you can blame me for it all my life. If we had not wasted all this time, we could have made the journey twice by now.'

Their father Israel said to them, 'If it must be so, then do this: in your baggage take, as a gift for the man, some of the produce for which our country is famous: a little balm and honey, with gum tragacanth, myrrh, pistachio nuts, and almonds. Take double the amount of silver with you and give back what was returned to you in your packs; perhaps there was some mistake. Take your brother with you and go straight back to the man. May God Almighty make him kindly disposed to you, and may he send back the one whom you left behind, and Benjamin too. As for me, if I am bereaved, I am bereaved.' So they took the gift and double the amount of silver, and accompanied by Benjamin they started at once for Egypt, where they presented themselves to Joseph.

When Joseph saw Benjamin with them, he said to his steward, 'Bring these men indoors; then kill a beast and prepare a meal, for they are to eat with me at midday.' He brought the men into Joseph's house as he had been ordered. They were afraid because they had been brought there; they thought, 'We have been brought in here because of that affair of the silver which was replaced in our packs the first time. He means to make some charge against us, to inflict punishment on us, seize our donkeys, and make us his slaves.' So they approached Joseph's steward and spoke to him at the door of the house. 'Please listen, my lord,' they said. 'After our first visit to buy food, when we reached the place where we were to spend the night, we opened our packs and each of us found his silver, the full amount of it, at the top of his pack. We have brought it back with us, and we have more silver to buy food. We do not know who put the silver in our packs.' He answered, 'Calm yourselves; do not be afraid. It must have been your God, the God of your father, who hid treasure for you in your packs. I did receive the silver.' Then he brought Simeon out to them.

The steward conducted them into Joseph's house and gave them water to bathe their feet, and provided feed for their donkeys. They had their gifts ready against Joseph's arrival at midday, for they had heard that they were to eat there. When he came into the house, they presented him with the gifts which they had brought, bowing to the ground before him. He asked them how they were and said, 'Is your father well, the old man of whom you spoke? Is he still alive?' 'Yes, my lord, our father is still alive and well,' they answered, bowing low in obeisance. When Joseph looked around he saw his own mother's son, his brother Benjamin, and asked, 'Is this your youngest brother, of whom you told me?' and to Benjamin he said, 'May God be gracious to you, my son!' Joseph, suddenly overcome by his feelings for his brother, was almost in tears, and he went into the inner room and wept. Then, having bathed his face, he came out and, with his feelings now under control, he ordered the meal to be served. He was served by himself, and the brothers by themselves; the Egyptians who were at the meal were also served separately, for to Egyptians it is abhorrent to eat with Hebrews. When at his direction the brothers were seated, the eldest first and so on down to the youngest, they looked at one another in astonishment. Joseph sent them each a portion from what was before him, but Benjamin's portion was five times larger than any of the others. So they feasted and drank with him.

Joseph gave the steward these instructions: 'Fill the men's packs with food, as much as they can carry, and put each man's silver at the top of his pack. And put my goblet, the silver one, at the top of the youngest brother's pack along with the silver for the grain.' He did as Joseph had told him. At first light the brothers were allowed to take their donkeys and set off; but before they had gone very far from the city, Joseph said to his steward, 'Go after those men at once, and when you catch up with them, say, "Why have you repaid good with evil? Why have you stolen the silver goblet? It is the one my lord drinks from, and which he uses for divination. This is a wicked thing you have done."' When the steward overtook them, he reported his master's words. But they replied, 'My lord, how can you say such things? Heaven forbid that we should do such a thing! Look! The silver we found at the top of our packs we brought back to you from Canaan. Why, then, should we steal silver or gold from your master's house? If any one of us is found with the goblet, he shall die; and, what is more, my lord, the rest of us shall become your slaves.' He said, 'Very well; I accept what you say. Only the one in whose possession it is found will become my slave; the rest will go free.' Each quickly lowered his pack to the ground and opened it, and when the steward searched, beginning with the eldest and finishing with the youngest, the goblet was found in Benjamin's pack.

JOSEPH FORGIVES HIS BROTHERS
Genesis 44:13 – 45:28

At this they tore their clothes; then one and all they loaded their donkeys and returned to the city.

Joseph was still in the house when Judah and his brothers arrived, and they threw themselves on the ground before him. Joseph said, 'What is this you have done? You might have known that a man such as I am uses divination.' Judah said, 'What can we say, my lord? What can we plead, or how can we clear ourselves? God has uncovered our crime. Here we are, my lord, ready to be made your slaves, we ourselves as well as the one who was found with the goblet.' 'Heaven forbid that I should do such a thing!' answered Joseph. 'Only the one who was found with the goblet shall become my slave; the rest of you can go home to your father safe and sound.'

Then Judah went up to him and said, 'Please listen, my lord, and let your servant speak a word, I beg. Do not be angry with me, for you are as great as Pharaoh himself. My lord, you asked us whether we had a father or a brother. We answered, "We have an aged father, and he has a young son born in his old age; this boy's full brother is dead, and since he alone is left of his mother's children, his father loves him." You said to us, your servants, "Bring him down to me so that I may set eyes on him." We told you, my lord, that the boy could not leave his father; his father would die if he left him. But you said, "Unless your youngest brother comes down with you, you shall not enter my presence again." We went back to your servant my father, and reported to him what your lordship had said, so when our father told us to go again and buy food, we answered, "We cannot go down; for without our youngest brother we cannot enter the man's presence; but if our brother is with us, we will go." Then your servant my father said to us, "You know that my wife bore me two sons. One left me, and I said, 'He must have been torn to pieces.' I have not seen him since. If you take this one from me as well, and he comes to any harm, then you will bring down my grey hairs in misery to the grave." Now, my lord, if I return to my father without the boy – and remember, his life is bound up with the boy's – what will happen is this: he will see that the boy is not with us and he will die, and your servants will have brought down our father's grey hairs in sorrow to the grave. Indeed, my lord, it was I who went surety for the boy to my father. I said, "If I do not bring him back to you, then you can blame me for it all my life." Now, my lord, let me remain in place of the boy as my lord's slave, and let him go with his brothers. How can I return to my father without the boy? I could not bear to see the misery which my father would suffer.'

Joseph was no longer able to control his feelings in front of all his attendants, and he called, 'Let everyone leave my presence!' There was nobody present when Joseph made himself known to his brothers, but he wept so loudly that the Egyptians heard him, and news of it got to Pharaoh's household. Joseph said to his brothers, 'I am Joseph! Can my father be still alive?' They were so dumbfounded at finding themselves face to face with Joseph that they could not answer. Joseph said to them, 'Come closer to me,' and when they did so, he said, 'I am your brother Joseph, whom you sold into Egypt.

177

Now do not be distressed or blame yourselves for selling me into slavery here; it was to save lives that God sent me ahead of you. For there have now been two years of famine in the land, and there will be another five years with neither ploughing nor harvest. God sent me on ahead of you to ensure that you will have descendants on earth, and to preserve for you a host of survivors. It is clear that it was not you who sent me here, but God, and he has made me Pharaoh's chief counsellor, lord over his whole household and ruler of all Egypt. Hurry back to my father and give him this message from his son Joseph: "God has made me lord of all Egypt. Come down to me without delay. You will live in the land of Goshen and be near me, you, your children and grandchildren, your flocks and herds, and all that you have. I shall provide for you there and see that you and your household and all that you have are not reduced to want; for there are still five years of famine to come." You can see for yourselves, and so can my brother Benjamin, that it is really Joseph himself who is speaking to you. Tell my father of all the honour which I enjoy in Egypt, tell him all you have seen, and bring him down here with all speed.' He threw his arms round his brother Benjamin and wept, and Benjamin too embraced him weeping. He then kissed each of his brothers and wept over them; after that his brothers were able to talk with him.

When the report reached the royal palace that Joseph's brothers had come, Pharaoh and his officials were pleased. Pharaoh told Joseph to say to his brothers: 'This is what you must do. Load your beasts and go straight back to Canaan. Fetch your father and your households and come to me. I shall give you the best region there is in Egypt, and you will enjoy the fat of the land.' He was also to tell them: 'Take wagons from Egypt for your dependants and your wives and fetch your father back here. Have no regrets at leaving your possessions, for all the best there is in the whole of Egypt is yours.'

Israel's sons followed these instructions, and Joseph supplied them with wagons, as Pharaoh had ordered, and provisions for the journey. To each of them he gave new clothes, but to Benjamin he gave three hundred pieces of silver and five sets of clothes. Moreover he sent his father ten donkeys carrying the finest products of Egypt, and ten she-donkeys laden with grain, bread, and other provisions for the journey. He sent his brothers on their way, warning them not to quarrel among themselves on the road. They set off, and went up from Egypt to their father Jacob in Canaan. When they told him that Joseph was still alive and was ruler of the whole of Egypt, he was stunned at the news and did not believe them. However when they reported to him all that Joseph had said to them, and when he saw the wagons which Joseph had provided to fetch him, his spirit revived. Israel said, 'It is enough! Joseph my son is still alive; I shall go and see him before I die.'

THE ISRAELITES SETTLE IN EGYPT
Genesis 46:1–5, 28–30; 47:1–10; 48:1–21; 49:29 – 50:26

Israel set out with all that he had and came to Beersheba, where he offered sacrifices to the God of his father Isaac. God called to Israel in a vision by night, 'Jacob! Jacob!' and he answered, 'I am here.' God said, 'I am God, the God of your father. Do not be afraid to go down to Egypt, for there I shall make you a great nation. I shall go down to Egypt with you, and I myself shall bring you back again without fail; and Joseph's will be the hands that close your eyes.' So Jacob set out from Beersheba. Israel's sons conveyed their father Jacob along with their wives and children in the wagons which Pharaoh had sent to bring him...

Jacob sent Judah ahead to Joseph to advise him that he was on his way to Goshen. They entered Goshen, and Joseph had his chariot yoked to go up there to meet Israel his father. When they met, Joseph threw his arms round him and wept on his shoulder for a long time. Israel said to Joseph, 'I have seen for myself that you are still alive. Now I am ready to die...'

Joseph came and reported to Pharaoh, 'My father and my brothers have arrived from Canaan, with their flocks and herds and everything they possess, and they are now in Goshen.' He had chosen five of his brothers, and he brought them into Pharaoh's presence. When he asked them what their occupation was, they answered, 'We are shepherds like our fathers before us, and we have come to stay in this country, because owing to the severe famine in Canaan there is no pasture there for our flocks. We ask your majesty's leave to settle now in Goshen.' Pharaoh said to Joseph, 'As to your father and your brothers who have come to you, the land of Egypt is at your disposal; settle them in the best part of it. Let them live in Goshen, and if you know of any among them with the skill, make them chief herdsmen in charge of my cattle.'

Then Joseph brought his father in and presented him to Pharaoh. Jacob blessed Pharaoh, who asked him his age, and he answered, 'The years of my life on earth are one hundred and thirty; few and hard have they been – fewer than the years my fathers lived.' Jacob then blessed Pharaoh and withdrew from his presence...

Some time later Joseph was informed that his father was ill, so he took his two sons, Manasseh and Ephraim, with him and came to Jacob. When Jacob heard that his son Joseph had come to him, he gathered his strength and sat up in bed. Jacob said to Joseph, 'God Almighty appeared to me at Luz in Canaan and blessed me; he said to me, "I shall make you fruitful and increase your descendants until they become a host of nations. I shall give this land to them after you as a possession for all time." Now,' Jacob went on, 'your two sons, who were born in Egypt before I came to join you here, will be counted as my sons; Ephraim and Manasseh will be mine as Reuben and Simeon are. But the children born to you after them will be counted as yours; in respect of their tribal territory they will be reckoned under their elder brothers' names. In Canaan on my return from Paddan-aram and while we were still some distance from Ephrath, your mother Rachel died on the way, and I buried her there by the road to Ephrath' (that is Bethlehem).

When Israel saw Joseph's sons, he said, 'Who are these?' 'They are my sons', replied Joseph, 'whom God has given me here.' Israel said, 'Then bring them to me, that I may bless them.' Now Israel's eyes were dim with age, and he could hardly see. Joseph brought the boys close to his father, and he kissed them and embraced them. He said to Joseph, 'I had not expected to see your face again, and now God has let me see your sons as well.' Joseph removed them from his father's knees and bowed to the ground. Then he took the two of them and brought them close to Israel: Ephraim on the right, that is Israel's left; and Manasseh on the left, that is Israel's right. But Israel, crossing his hands, stretched out his right hand and laid it on Ephraim's head, although he was the younger, and laid his left hand on Manasseh's head, even though he was the firstborn. He blessed Joseph and said:

> The God in whose presence my forefathers lived,
> my forefathers Abraham and Isaac,
> the God who has been my shepherd all my life to this day,
> the angel who rescued me from all misfortune,
> may he bless these boys;
> they will be called by my name,
> and by the names of my forefathers, Abraham and Isaac;
> may they grow into a great people on earth.

When Joseph saw his father laying his right hand on Ephraim's head, he was displeased and took hold of his father's hand to move it from Ephraim's head to Manasseh's. He said, 'That is not right, father. This is the firstborn; lay your right hand on his head.' But his father refused; he said, 'I know, my son, I know. He too will become a people, and he too will become great. Yet his younger brother will be greater than he, and his descendants will be a whole nation in themselves.' So he blessed them that day and said:

> When a blessing is pronounced in Israel,
> men shall use your names and say,
> 'May God make you like Ephraim and Manasseh.'

So he set Ephraim before Manasseh. Then Israel said to Joseph... 'I am about to be gathered to my ancestors; bury me with my forefathers in the cave on the plot of land which belonged to Ephron the Hittite, that is the cave on the plot of land at Machpelah east of Mamre in Canaan, the field which Abraham bought from Ephron the Hittite for a burial-place. There Abraham was buried with his wife Sarah; there Isaac and his wife Rebecca were buried; and that is where I buried Leah. The land and the cave there were bought from the Hittites.' When Jacob had finished giving these instructions... he drew up his feet on to the bed, breathed his last, and was gathered to his ancestors.

Then Joseph threw himself upon his father, weeping over him

and kissing him. He gave orders to the physicians in his service to embalm his father, and they did so, finishing the task in forty days, the usual time required for embalming. The Egyptians mourned Israel for seventy days. When the period of mourning was over, Joseph spoke to members of Pharaoh's household: 'May I ask a favour – please speak for me to Pharaoh. Tell him that my father on his deathbed made me swear that I would bury him in the grave that he had bought for himself in Canaan. Ask Pharaoh to let me go up and bury my father; and afterwards I shall return.' Pharaoh's reply was: 'Go and bury your father in accordance with your oath.' So Joseph went up to bury his father, and with him went all Pharaoh's officials, the elders of his household, and all the elders of Egypt, as well as all Joseph's own household, his brothers, and his father's household; only their children, with the flocks and herds, were left in Goshen. Chariots as well as horsemen went up with him, a very great company.

When they came to the threshing-floor of Atad beside the river Jordan, they raised a loud and bitter lamentation; and Joseph observed seven days' mourning for his father. When the Canaanites who lived there saw this mourning at the threshing-floor of Atad, they said, 'How bitterly the Egyptians are mourning!' So they named the place beside the Jordan Abel-mizraim.

Thus Jacob's sons did to him as he had instructed them: they took him to Canaan and buried him in the cave on the plot of land at Machpelah, the land which Abraham had bought as a burial-place from Ephron the Hittite, to the east of Mamre. After burying his father, Joseph returned to Egypt with his brothers and all who had gone up with him for the burial.

Now that their father was dead, Joseph's brothers were afraid, for they said, 'What if Joseph should bear a grudge against us and pay us back for all the harm we did to him?' They therefore sent a messenger to Joseph to say, 'In his last words to us before he died, your father gave us this message: "Say this to Joseph: I ask you to forgive your brothers' crime and wickedness; I know they did you harm." So now we beg you: forgive our crime, for we are servants of your father's God.' Joseph was moved to tears by their words. His brothers approached and bowed to the ground before him. 'We are your slaves,' they said. But Joseph replied, 'Do not be afraid. Am I in the place of God? You meant to do me harm; but God meant to bring good out of it by preserving the lives of many people, as we see today. Do not be afraid. I shall provide for you and your dependants.' Thus he comforted them and set their minds at rest.

Joseph remained in Egypt, he and his father's household. He lived to be a hundred and ten years old, and saw Ephraim's children to the third generation; he also recognized as his the children of Manasseh's son Machir. He said to his brothers, 'I am about to die; but God will not fail to come to your aid and take you from here to the land which he promised on oath to Abraham, Isaac, and Jacob.' He made the sons of Israel solemnly swear that when God came to their aid, they would carry his bones up with them from there. So Joseph died in Egypt at the age of a hundred and ten, and he was embalmed and laid in a coffin.

Index of Primary Sources